cognitive behavioral therapy for depression

MONIQUE THOMPSON, PSYD

cognitive behavioral therapy for depression

Essential Strategies to Manage Negative Thoughts and Start Living Your Life

ROCKRIDGE
PRESS

For general information on our other products and services or to obtain technical support, please contact our Customer Care Department within the United States at (866) 744-2665, or outside the United States at (510) 253-0500.

Rockridge Press publishes its books in a variety of electronic and print formats. Some content that appears in print may not be available in electronic books, and vice versa.

Interior and Cover Designer: Rachel Haeseker
Art Producer: Karen Williams
Editors: Seth Schwartz and Nora Spiegel
Production Editor: Andrew Yackira

Photography used under license from Shutterstock.com. Author photo courtesy of Kirsten Lara Getchell.

ISBN: Print 978-1-64739-100-3 | eBook 978-1-64739-034-1
R0

To Simone and Katya, who have been my greatest supporters and encouraged me to finish this book during the challenges we all faced during the COVID-19 crisis. And to Oliver for his expansive love, support, and inspiration.

contents

INTRODUCTION VIII

Part One: Understanding Your Depression 1
Chapter 1: Dealing with Depression 3
Chapter 2: Depression Self-Assessment 21

Part Two: Identify Your Thoughts 27
Chapter 3: Think Different 29
Chapter 4: Change Your Internal Beliefs 47

Part Three: Connect with Your Feelings 65
Chapter 5: Deal with Your Emotions 67
Chapter 6: Be Mindful 85

Part Four: Change Your Behaviors 99
Chapter 7: Be Goal Oriented 101
Chapter 8: Act Now 113

Part Five: Stay Engaged 131
Chapter 9: Treat Yourself 133
Chapter 10: Stay the Course 145

RESOURCES 155 / APPENDIX 158 / REFERENCES 159 / INDEX 165

introduction

If you have picked up this book, you are likely struggling with yourself and your life in some way. Maybe you find it hard to get out of bed in the morning, or to focus at work, or to find motivation to do much of anything. Maybe you have found yourself withdrawing from family and friends, despite how lonely you may feel. Maybe you are turning to food or alcohol or drugs to make the pain go away. Maybe you haven't felt joy in a long time. You are looking for answers, relief, tools—something to help you move beyond the shadow cast by depression's dark cloud.

First, know that you are not alone. The National Institute of Mental Health estimated that nearly 16.2 million people experienced a depressive episode in 2016—that's nearly 1 in 7 people in the United States.

Second, know that it is an act of courage to just open this book and take this first step in getting help. I hope that using this book will be one of many actions you take to begin to move toward understanding and managing your depression with the empirically validated strategies and techniques laid out in this book. Cognitive behavioral therapy (CBT) for depression has helped innumerable people improve their moods and reengage with the things that matter to them, and I sincerely believe you can be one of those people.

I was very pleased when I was asked to write this book on cognitive behavioral therapy for depression, because I have spent much of my career practicing and researching CBT for depression, anxiety, and insomnia, and I am passionate about helping people find the tools they need to improve their own lives. Early in my career, I took a position at the Golden Bear Sleep and Mood Research Clinic at UC Berkeley as a member of a development team working on enhancing CBT treatment for depression. This allowed me to develop a deep understanding of CBT for depression, and the broad array of strategies and skills that can be learned and practiced to manage and improve depression symptoms. I have continued to specialize in CBT for depression as a partner at the San Francisco Bay Area Center for Cognitive Therapy.

My interest in how depression works and treatments that allow people to manage their symptoms is also personal. During a particularly difficult time in my life, I became aware that I was experiencing the pervasive negative thinking and difficulty mobilizing that I had learned so much about in my doctoral studies and clinical training. As a postdoctoral student in clinical psychology, there was something almost fascinating in recognizing that I was having the distorted negative thinking and feelings of hopelessness that characterize a major depressive episode. I knew about the treatments that were effective for depression and was able to get the support that I needed to move through the episode and back into my life. Despite how painful that period was, I have always been grateful to have had the personal experience of depression to inform my work with my patients, and as I write this book on CBT for depression.

CBT is a treatment that is proven to be effective at improving and managing depression. It has evolved to incorporate mindfulness and acceptance practices that support more effective and flexible ways for us to relate to our emotional lives. This book can be used as a self-help guide that will help you to understand depression and provide you with strategies that can help you improve your symptoms, or it can be used with a therapist. Depression is a unique experience for every person, and the examples I have offered won't cover every symptom or describe any one person's experience exactly. Some of the chapters and strategies will seem more relevant to your particular experience, and you should feel free to focus on those strategies more. If you find that it is difficult to integrate these strategies into your life, or you need extra help doing so, I encourage you to seek out the support of a therapist.

This book focuses on simple, actionable strategies and tools for helping you to feel better. I encourage you to begin now, and to allow yourself to be open and curious about what this book has to offer you. The challenges you are facing today are likely to look very different with time and effort. It is natural to get discouraged at times, and if you find that you lose momentum or are not doing the exercise and practices outlined in the book, remember that the goal is progress, not perfection. Just opening the book, reading a few paragraphs, or trying one of the strategies is a step toward feeling better. Reading and using the strategies outlined in this book may feel like work, but it is actually an investment in yourself and your ability to navigate the ups and downs that all of us encounter in our lives. Consider the time that you spend with this book to be a gift that you are giving yourself.

I have found in my personal and professional experience that it is more helpful to think of depression as something you do rather than something that you have. This perspective recognizes that there are many ways to take action to change the way you feel. I hope you will use the skills and strategies in this book to find your way back to the things in life that matter to you, feeling confident in your ability to understand and manage your depression.

Part One

Understanding Your Depression

CBT for depression is an empirically validated treatment that is proven to be very effective for reducing the symptoms of depression and developing skills and strategies that will enable you to relate to your emotions more effectively. In the next two chapters, you will learn what depression looks like, how it is maintained, and how it is treated. You will also learn how to use a simple symptom questionnaire to track your progress as you make your way through the exercises and strategies in this book.

chapter 1

dealing with depression

Many people struggle with feelings of depression at some point in their lives, and depression is experienced by all types of people, at any age, and under many circumstances. If you have been depressed, you know it is much more than simply having a low mood or "feeling blue." It can feel over-powering and overwhelming, like a heavy weight you just can't escape from. The world can seem to lose its color and turn dull and gray. You may feel tired, empty, and hopeless, and lose touch with the things that matter to you. You may lose interest in doing things you used to love, or you may push away the people you care about. Depression is so much more than just feeling sad.

The good news is depression is one of the most common mood disorders, and is highly treatable. In this chapter, we will explore some of these treatments and get you started on using the tools of cognitive behavioral therapy to manage your depression and find relief, so you can live your life more fully.

JACK had worked really hard to finish his degree in engineering and get a job at a start-up company. Saddled with debt from student loans, Jack worked long hours and stayed out late drinking to "fit in" and to impress his coworkers. Jack had always struggled to make friends and considered himself to be an "oddball." It took him a long time to make a few friends at college, and he missed the easy camaraderie he had with his small social group. He had struggled with mood swings in college and did some therapy at the counseling center that had been helpful. He learned that he could manage his mood when he took care of himself by eating right, exercising, and getting enough sleep.

Jack didn't think that he had time for this kind of self-care in his new job, and just decided to "push through." The long workdays and late nights took a toll on Jack; he found that he was feeling more anxious at work, and worried a lot about what his boss and coworkers thought about him. He was convinced that he wasn't as smart as the other people on his team and that he wasn't going to be able meet the expectations of his boss. He began getting to work late and skipping meetings to avoid contact with his boss. He worried that his boss would notice and he would be fired. When his boss noticed that he seemed a little down, his boss suggested that Jack take a few days to "take care of himself." Jack concluded that this was his boss telling him that he needed to "shape up or ship out," making him feel even worse. His new relationship was getting more serious, but he worried that his lack of energy and lack of interest in sex would cause her to want to break things off. He didn't talk to anyone about how he felt because he didn't want to "be a downer."

Life Under a Dark Cloud

Depression is a word that is used to describe a human experience that many of us will encounter in our lifetime. It is estimated that 7 percent of the US population is experiencing clinical depression at any given moment (Kessler et al. 2005). Nearly one in three women and one in five men will experience depression (National Institute of Mental Health 2013), but no depression looks or feels the same. You are not alone, and there are decades of research to help you find your way out from under the dark cloud of depression and back into a rich, meaningful life.

Common Symptoms of Depression

People experiencing a depressed mood may feel sad, hopeless, or empty and have little interest in life or formerly pleasurable activities. Some people report feelings of irritability and anger or have physical symptoms such as fatigue, achiness, headaches, and stomach upset. Symptoms of depression can range from mild to severe and include:

Feelings of worthlessness and guilt: When you are depressed, you may lose sight of the things that give your life meaning and purpose. You may also feel that the negative things in your life are your fault, and feel guilt or remorse.

Being slowed down or physically agitated: People who are experiencing depression often report that normal life activities feel very difficult, like they are "walking through mud" just doing ordinary things. Others feel an increased state of arousal and agitation that may take the form of irritability or angry outbursts.

Difficulties thinking, concentrating, or making decisions: Depression can impair your thinking and problem-solving abilities. Some people feel like they are "living in a fog" and find it difficult to focus on daily life tasks.

Overeating or undereating: When you are depressed, you may find that you are less hungry and find food unappealing. In contrast, some find that they eat more than usual and crave fatty and sugary foods.

Sleeping too much or too little: Many people with depression report difficulties falling and staying asleep. Others find that they are sleeping much more than usual.

Low energy or fatigue: When you are depressed, you may feel more tired and less able to mobilize.

Thoughts of death or suicide: Many people with depression report having thoughts of death or other morbid thoughts. Thoughts of self-harm and suicide can also accompany a depressive episode.

Depression can be a chronic disorder that may have periods of relief, and then come back again later during the course of a person's life. It can be a response to situational triggers such as increased stress, a recent trauma or loss, or a major life transition. It can also be related to negative past experiences such as childhood trauma or family dysfunction. The symptoms can range from mild to severe, and can be accompanied by additional symptoms such as anxiety, insomnia, and other psychiatric disorders.

When we are depressed, people often tell us to "buck up" or to stop being so negative. The Western world values extroversion and optimism, and this cultural attitude contributes to the misconception that depression is a character flaw or weakness, which can worsen the shame and hopelessness experienced during depression. People who have struggled with depression know that getting out of it is not as easy or simple as just "cheering up." Depression is more complicated than that, and luckily research has helped us understand the complex factors that contribute to it.

IMPORTANT MESSAGE: If you are having thoughts of suicide or self-harm, please seek immediate medical care. You can call your medical doctor, go directly to your nearest emergency room, or call the National Suicide Prevention Lifeline, 1-800-273-8255.

Factors That Contribute to Depression

Research has helped us understand that depression is a "bio-psycho-social disorder," which means it is a culmination of biological, psychological, and environmental influences. This means that depression is linked to genetics and other biological factors, psychological factors such as childhood experiences and personality traits, and situational and environmental stressors. By identifying our own unique configurations of these factors of depression, we can begin to find our way out of it.

This list outlines the three main factors that contribute to depression:

Bio: People with genetic relatives who experience depression are more likely to experience depression. Chemicals in the brain, hormones, and other physiological factors can have an impact on how we think and feel.

Psycho: Early experiences or trauma can impact psychological processes and lead to depression later in life. Personality traits such as negative affectivity (pessimism) also play a role in the development of depression.

Social: Situational factors such as stress in the home, relationships, economic stressors, and substance use contribute to depression. People may also experience depression as a result of oppression based on race, sexual orientation or gender identity, and other marginalized identities.

What Depression Is and Is Not

Depression is different from feelings of sadness or grief. Sadness and grief are normal responses to difficult situations such as the end of a relationship, the death of a loved one, or an unexpected job loss. A person experiencing sadness or grief in these situations is going through a natural process of coming to terms with difficult life circumstances, and will likely move through them with time. However, these situations may lead to depression if the individual is unable to process the loss and reenter into meaningful life activities.

Depression impacts every area of our lives, including how we think, feel, and behave. This constellation of behaviors, thoughts, feelings, and situational factors culminates in maladaptive and unhelpful coping strategies, such as experiential avoidance, emotional numbing, and social withdrawal. Oddly, when we are depressed, our brains tell us to do the opposite of what would make us feel better. The depressed mind urges us to isolate ourselves from our friends and family members; to engage in unhealthy numbing behaviors like drugs or alcohol, overeating, or excessive sleeping; and to avoid pleasurable experiences beyond the cloud of depression. Depression leaves us feeling lost, with no road map to lead us back into our lives.

We generally talk about depression as something we "feel" or "have," but in this book we will emphasize a more accurate and empowering perspective: depression is also something we "do," and therefore something we can make efforts to do differently. Researchers have been able to isolate certain behaviors and thinking errors that reinforce and maintain depression. For example, people who are depressed are more likely to see in black-and-white or all-or-nothing terms, such as "I always screw up" or "she will never love me." Another thinking error is the inclination to "catastrophize" situations, predicting that all situations will ultimately lead to the worst-case scenario. These behaviors and thinking errors lead people away from the things in their lives that bring them purpose and meaning, and into the dark terrain of negative thoughts, emotional numbness, and experiential avoidance. This book will help you to understand depression and how it works. It will also give you strategies to counter the negative thinking and experiential avoidance that perpetuate depression.

Types of Depression

Depression is a term that refers to a cluster of symptoms and behaviors. A list of the most common forms of depression is outlined here. It's important to note that some people who experience depression will also have co-occurring mood disorders, such as bipolar disorder, post-traumatic stress disorder, and anxiety disorders, and I encourage you to get specific help for those if that is the case.

Major Depressive Disorder (MDD): This is the most common form of depression. People with MDD may feel down most days and lose interest in daily activities for a period of two weeks or more. Five other symptoms of depression must also be present.

Persistent Depressive Disorder (PDD): While MDD symptoms fluctuate across time, PDD is a more chronic form of depression. PDD is diagnosed if a person feels persistently depressed for at least two years. Two other symptoms of depression must also be present. It is sometimes called "dysthymia."

Situational Depression: Situational depression usually emerges from an experience of stress or trauma, and is considered to be a type of adjustment disorder. Sometimes referred to as "reactive depression," this type of depression makes it hard to respond or adjust to life after the stressful experience.

Atypical Depression: Despite its name, atypical depression is actually one of the most prevalent forms of depression. This subtype of depression is characterized by weight gain, excessive sleeping, and fatigue. One of the main things that distinguishes it from typical depression is that a person still has "mood reactivity," which means they are able to respond to positive events with a bright mood.

Seasonal Affective Disorder (SAD): SAD is a type of depression that corresponds with changes in seasons. Usually, people with SAD will experience increased fatigue, negative thinking, and moodiness in the fall and winter, and decreased fatigue, negative thinking, and moodiness in the spring and summer.

Postpartum Depression (PPD): PPD is distinguished from the "baby blues" experienced by nearly 80 percent of people who just gave birth, in that the symptoms are much more severe and last at least two weeks. PPD symptoms begin during pregnancy or after the birth of the child and are experienced by nearly 8 percent of people who have recently given birth.

Premenstrual Dysphoric Disorder (PMDD): PMDD differs from PMS and common mood fluctuations during the menstrual cycle in that it includes more serious forms of anxiety, irritability, intense mood swings, and physical symptoms that greatly interfere with a person's life. This diagnosis is currently not widely accepted or used.

What You Can Do about Your Depression

One of the most cunning lies depression tells us is that there is no hope, and that there are no solutions for the problems we face. But depression is one of the most well researched and understood mental disorders, and cognitive behavioral therapy is the best understood and most empirically validated treatment for depression. CBT has been found to be as effective as antidepressant medication in many cases, and there is evidence that CBT in addition to antidepressant medication may be more effective in more severe cases of depression (Driessen and Hollon 2010). This book will outline a treatment for depression that is the result of decades of empirical research and clinical practice. CBT for depression is the gold standard treatment for depression and has been found to be effective for many people; I hope that you will find information and strategies that can help you, too.

CBT was developed by Dr. Aaron Beck, considered the father of CBT, in the 1960s. He observed that his depressed patients experienced persistent streams of negative thoughts. These "automatic thoughts" focused on three domains: thoughts of the self, the world, and the future. Beck was intrigued by how these patients' thoughts seemed so biased toward the negative interpretations that maintained their depressed mood. He experimented with methods to challenge these thoughts and their underlying beliefs, so that his patients could view situations more realistically. He noticed that when his patients were able to change their negative thoughts and beliefs, their mood improved (Beck 2011). Around the same time period, Albert Ellis was exploring behavioral interventions for treating mental disorders. The work of Beck, Ellis, and others has resulted in CBT and other empirically validated treatments. A third "wave" of CBT introduced new concepts and terms to the broader CBT repertoire, including mindfulness, self-compassion, psychological flexibility, and acceptance. The newer CBT modalities include mindfulness-based cognitive therapy (MBCT), dialectical behavior therapy (DBT), and acceptance and commitment therapy (ACT) (Hayes et al. 2013).

What Is CBT?

CBT is an action-oriented and goal-focused therapy that conceptualizes depression as the consequence of what we think, do, and feel. Sounds simple, right? Researchers have developed tools and strategies to help you evaluate and change your thoughts and behaviors in order to improve your depressive symptoms, and more recent CBT therapies integrate mindfulness and self-compassion practices to help you learn to relate to your thoughts and mood in a more flexible and resilient way (Dobson 2008). CBT stands out from other therapies because of its time-limited scope and focus on the here and now. It has been validated through hundreds of clinical trials that determined which skills and concepts are most helpful to people in improving their symptoms.

The core characteristics of cognitive behavioral therapy are:

Goal oriented: CBT focuses on specific goals for treatment that the therapist and client determine at the beginning of therapy. These goals will guide the course and content of the treatment.

Time limited: CBT is not meant to be a long-term therapy. A CBT treatment plan will include an estimate of the number of sessions that will be needed to achieve the treatment goals laid out at the beginning of therapy.

Concentrates on the here and now: CBT emphasizes what is happening currently rather than what has happened in the past. This does not mean that the therapy will not address experiences, circumstances, and beliefs from the past; these things will be considered as a way to understand current life situations and experiences.

Figure 1.1 is a simplified version of the CBT model that I show to my patients when we begin to conceptualize their particular cases of depression. I explain that the CBT models allow us to conceptualize depression as the consequence of the interaction of the three

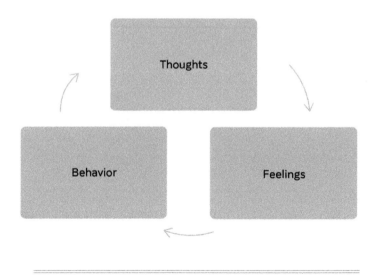

Figure 1.1 The CBT Model: The thoughts-behavior-feelings cycle

domains represented in the model: thoughts, behaviors, and feelings. CBT hinges on the idea that these three domains are interrelated, and a change in one domain can impact the others. For instance, changing our thinking can change how we feel and behave. In this book, you will learn strategies that will allow you to use the CBT model to manage your depression and go back to living a full life. In the last chapters, we will discuss how to manage relapses when they occur. What I find so helpful and hopeful about conceptualizing depression with this model is that we are immediately flagging that there are at least three different places to intervene in order to move toward feeling better. Each of these three domains are interconnected, so intervening in one area is likely to impact other areas on the model.

For instance, when Jack is feeling depressed and low in energy, he makes decisions like skipping meetings, which he justifies by negative thoughts like "They don't care if I'm there. They think I'm a loser" (see figure 1.2). If Jack changes his behavior by attending rather than missing the meetings, he is likely to feel less guilty and worried, and may have experiences with his boss and coworkers that make him feel less insecure about his job and team (see figure 1.3).

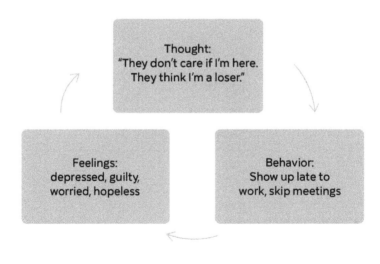

Figure 1.2 The CBT Model: How negative thoughts influence behavior and feelings

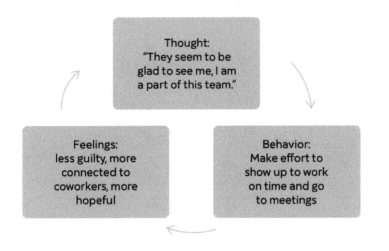

Figure 1.3 The CBT Model: How positive thoughts influence behavior and feelings

The CBT model helps structure the way we understand and treat depression. By becoming more aware of the maladaptive thoughts and behaviors that perpetuate the depressive cycle, we are able to use the skills and concepts in this book to shift to alternative thoughts and behaviors.

Initially, CBT focuses on the negative thoughts that are a part of depression, and teaches you skills to challenge them. These may be thoughts like "I am worthless," "Nobody likes me," "This is too hard," "I can't do it," and "I'm going to feel this bad forever." These thoughts are likely to lead you to behave in ways that perpetuate the negative thinking.

We will also focus on how your behaviors are impacting your mood. One of the most unhelpful behaviors associated with depression is "experiential avoidance," or avoiding experiences that seem difficult or uncomfortable. Experiential avoidance can take many forms: avoiding contact with friends and family, or missing work or important events. Believing our negative thoughts and acting as if they are true creates a vicious cycle that feeds our depression symptoms.

Thoughts are often the first place to intervene when we want to begin to explore ways to help ourselves feel better. Becoming more aware of our thinking and how it can influence our mood and behavior is the core skill of CBT therapy. How do we "catch," or recognize, negative thoughts

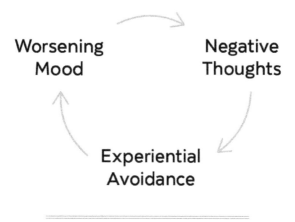

Worsening Mood

Negative Thoughts

Experiential Avoidance

Figure 1.4 Experiential Avoidance Cycle

so we can become aware that we are entering this negative cycle? The first step is being able to realize that *you are not your thoughts.* Thoughts are words and ideas that your brain generates, but they are not you. You are able to become aware of these thoughts and decide which ones to attend to and which to let go of or modify.

For instance, Jack assumes that his friends will think he is a "downer," so he stops going out with them. This thought leads him to feel more alone and isolated and keeps him from having experiences that will debunk the thought that his friends will think he is a downer. CBT therapy helped Jack learn to evaluate these negative thoughts before he acted on them. In chapter 3, you will learn to use CBT tools to examine your thoughts and look for evidence to confirm or disprove them before acting on them.

Cultivating skills for and knowledge about managing our moods and how we relate to our emotional experiences is a lifelong pursuit. This book will be a good way to begin or continue this important work, which will likely lead to a richer and more meaningful life. CBT provides skills and perspectives that are helpful for people in dealing with depression, but these skills are also life skills that can help you respond to all of life's stressors with resilience and flexibility.

Medications That Treat Depression

There are several types of medicine that have been found to be helpful for treating depression. Your medical doctor or therapist may recommend that you consult with a psychiatrist to evaluate if medication may be a good addition to your treatment plan. While research has shown that medication and therapy together is most effective for some types of depression, that is not true for all cases (Hollon et al. 2014). Many people are able to manage their symptoms without medication. Some people are concerned about side effects, or that they will become dependent on medications, or that medication will "change" them in some fundamental way. Discuss your concerns and questions about medications with your medical doctor or psychiatrist.

You may need to try several different medications before you find one that helps with your symptoms. You and your doctor will consider the symptoms you are having and potential side effects of different medications, and will determine which medication to try first. It is important to be patient and to communicate with your prescribing physician if you are experiencing side effects. Common side effects of these medications include stomach upset, increased appetite, sexual dysfunction, and fatigue. It can be useful for your doctor to know what medications have been helpful to other members of your family. Types of antidepressant medication include:

Selective Serotonin Reuptake Inhibitors (SSRIs): These are often the first medications that your doctor will try, because they tend to have fewer side effects and are well researched for effectiveness. The most common SSRIs include citalopram (Celexa), fluoxetine (Prozac), paroxetine (Paxil), and escitalopram (Lexapro).

Serotonin and Norepinephrine Reuptake Inhibitors (SNRIs): These include duloxetine (Cymbalta), venlafaxine (Effexor), desvenlafaxine (Pristiq), and levomilnacipran (Fetzima).

Atypical Antidepressants: These medications may be prescribed when other medications are not working, or for people diagnosed with atypical depression. Atypical antidepressants include: mirtazapine (Remeron), vortioxetine (Trintellix), vilazodone (Viibryd), trazodone, and bupropion (Wellbutrin SR, Wellbutrin XL). Bupropion is often favored because it has a low incidence of sexual side effects and weight gain.   →

Tricyclic Antidepressants: Tricyclic antidepressants are associated with a greater risk of side effects and will not be prescribed until other anti-depressants have been tried. Examples of medications in this category include nortriptyline (Pamelor), imipramine (Tofranil), amitriptyline, desipramine (Norpramin), and doxepin.

Monoamine Oxidase Inhibitors (MAOIs): These medications may be pre-scribed if other medications have not worked. Dietary changes are necessary, as MAOI medications can cause serious side effects. Examples of these medications include phenelzine (Nardil), tranylcypromine (Parnate), and isocarboxazid (Marplan). These medications cannot be prescribed with SSRIs.

How This Book Will Help

This book is designed to be used, on your own or with a therapist, to begin to address your depression systematically using CBT strategies and techniques. Because your version of depression is unique, this book has been designed to allow you to move freely between chapters and utilize the skills and concepts that are most relevant and helpful to you. That being said, an important part of the effectiveness of CBT is the psychoeducational component of the treatment. Try to read the chapters so that you can gain an understanding of what depression is, how it functions, what feeds it, and what steers it away from negative thoughts and unhealthy behaviors.

There are many opportunities for you to apply the skills and strategies of CBT in your daily life. Practice is a critical ingredient in the effectiveness of CBT. Do the exercises in this book and try to apply them as often as you can throughout the day. If you find that it is difficult to get yourself to read or do the exercises, consider finding a CBT therapist or other mental health provider to support you. While understanding the concepts of CBT is important, applying them in your daily life is the "active ingredient" in CBT. As I will emphasize throughout this book, depression is better understood as something you do rather than something you have. This doesn't mean that the depression is your fault, but it points to the fact that you will need to do something differently in order to move through this difficult time. And by picking up and reading this book, you have already started! Reaching out for support and professional advice shows that you are proactively trying to feel better.

While it can be very beneficial to read the entire book, it is not necessary to commit to completing the entire book in order to benefit. Some of you may just need to pick up a few helpful tips to apply in your daily life, while others will benefit from going through the book chapter by chapter to learn and apply many of the strategies. If you are particularly interested in the topic of a particular chapter, it is fine to read ahead and practice the skills out of order. The evidence-based strategies in this book address a wide variety of depression symptoms. Feel free to jump around and focus on the areas that are troubling you most.

Many of the mindfulness skills require you to set aside time to write or breathe or meditate. Many of these exercises may feel awkward or odd at first. Tap into your curiosity and desire for change to motivate yourself to give these strategies a try. These exercises are based on extensive empirical research and can be a critical part of your recovery. If you find it difficult to meditate without guidance, please consider using some of the guided meditation resources listed in the resource section in the back of the book.

Key Takeaways

- Many people struggle with feelings of depression at some point in their life.

- Depression is one of the most common mental disorders and is highly treatable.

- Nearly 1 in 3 women and 1 in 5 men will experience depression, but no depression looks or feels the same.

- CBT focuses on the negative automatic thoughts that are a part of depression and teaches you skills to challenge them.

- Believing our negative thoughts and acting as if they are true creates a vicious cycle that feeds our depression symptoms.

- One of the most unhelpful behaviors associated with depression is "experiential avoidance," which means avoiding experiences like contact with friends and family or missing work or important events.

- With practice you will be able to become aware of these thoughts and decide which ones to attend to and which ones to let go of or modify.

chapter 2

depression self-assessment

No depression looks or feels the same. An important part of working on your depression is to begin to really understand your unique depression profile and to note how it changes over time. One way that you will do this is by using a list of common depression symptoms to rate the symptoms that you are currently experiencing. This will give you a picture of your depression symptoms now and how they change as you use the strategies outlined in this book to address your depression. You may have many of these symptoms, or just a few. Your answers may change from one day to the next. We will use the questionnaire and our curiosity to begin investigating your unique version of depression to help you choose the strategies that may be most helpful.

Depression Questionnaire

Focusing on the past week, rate the severity of each symptom from zero to five (zero meaning "not at all in the last week," and five meaning "symptom experienced most days in the last week").

1. Feeling sad, down, or depressed

    0   1   2   3   4   5

2. Diminished interest or pleasure in life activities (this symptom must be present for a diagnosis)

    0   1   2   3   4   5

3. Significant weight change or appetite disturbance

    0   1   2   3   4   5

4. Sleep disturbance (too much or little)

    0   1   2   3   4   5

5. Overactive movement and restlessness, or slowing down and lack of movement

    0   1   2   3   4   5

6. Fatigue or lack of energy

    0   1   2   3   4   5

7. Feelings of worthlessness

    0   1   2   3   4   5

8. Diminished ability to concentrate and/or make decisions

    0   1   2   3   4   5

9. Thoughts of death or suicide

    0   1   2   3   4   5

It is important to recognize that the depression questionnaire is not a diagnostic tool. If you want to be assessed to determine whether you meet criteria for a diagnosis of clinical depression, you need to consult a trained mental health professional or your medical doctor.

As you use this book, complete this questionnaire once a week and record your score. It is best if you do it at regular intervals and times, for instance, every Sunday evening before bed rather than just at times when you are feeling particularly depressed. Recording these results over time will allow you to track changes in your symptoms as you make your way through the skills and strategies in this book.

You may notice that your scores stay the same, or that they change every week. If you notice that your scores are going down most weeks, this could mean that the skills and concepts you are applying from the book (in addition to other factors) are improving your mood. You could also compare your answers on the current questionnaire to the last one you completed to track whether you are improving on particular symptoms from one week to the next. For instance, Pam filled out the questionnaire weekly for the first four weeks and found that her scores on items one and two came down from threes to ones fairly quickly. She could see that the skills she had learned to challenge her negative thoughts were improving her mood and ability to engage with her life.

If you notice that your symptoms consistently go up or don't change at all, this may indicate that you should consult with a medical professional about other treatment options.

As you get in the habit of completing the depression questionnaire weekly, you might begin to notice that there are certain items that you always rate highly and others that you rate low or don't experience at all. The items on this questionnaire that you score higher on will help guide you toward the chapters and strategies that will be most helpful to you.

For instance, Pam noticed that she always scored the items about sleep (question 4) and fatigue (question 6) as fours or fives, even as her mood began to improve in other areas. She found her scores on these items improved once she worked through the strategy in chapter 9 to identify and eliminate activities that made her feel worse, and when she started using specific self-care strategies outlined in that chapter.

Key Takeaways

- No depression looks or feels the same.

- The depression questionnaire will help you understand the specific symptoms and concerns that you are experiencing.

- Filling out the depression questionnaire each week will help you see how your symptoms change across time as you work your way through the strategies in this book.

- If you notice that your scores are going down most weeks, this may indicate that you are doing things in your life, including working with this book, that are improving your symptoms.

- If you notice that your symptoms consistently go up or don't change at all, this may indicate that you should consult with a medical professional about other treatment options.

- Using this questionnaire to begin investigating your unique version of depression will help empower you to choose the strategies that may be most helpful for you.

- This type of questionnaire is an invaluable resource for you to understand your symptoms and track your progress as you develop skills and strategies for managing depression.

Part Two

Identify Your Thoughts

One of the core concepts and practices of CBT focuses on our thoughts and how they influence our behavior and feelings. Understanding and recognizing the relationship among these three things is a core skill that will allow you to manage your emotions in a different way. Our thoughts are often linked to deeper beliefs about ourselves, others, and the world, that we developed during childhood and other important periods in our lives. The next two chapters will focus on strategies that will allow you to identify your negative thoughts and recognize how they are impacting your actions (behavior) and mood (feelings). Then you will learn how you can balance your thinking to be more accurate and helpful. Once you have mastered this core skill, you will examine the internal beliefs that are feeding your thoughts and consider how you can address them and create more accurate and helpful beliefs about yourself, the world, and others.

chapter 3

think different

The feelings that accompany depression, such as guilt, worthlessness, fatigue, and feeling overwhelmed, can sometimes feel like they come "out of nowhere," but research has helped us understand that our feelings generally arise from thoughts we are having about ourselves, others, and the world (Beck 2005). When we become aware of our thoughts, the negative feelings that are a part of depression begin to make a lot more sense. These thoughts are incredibly powerful mediators of our experience, yet when we examine them, they are often inaccurate and unhelpful. The first step toward changing how you feel is beginning to identify the thoughts that underlie your mood.

DIANE was a 63-year-old woman who lived with her three beloved dogs and husband of 40 years. Her children were grown and out of the house, living adult lives. She had retired from her job six months earlier and had looked forward to traveling more, walking daily, and volunteering. She suffered an injury to her leg that limited her mobility and ability to engage in the active lifestyle she had always enjoyed. Diane's painful injury curtailed her retirement plans. She found herself stuck at home, or spending her days going to tedious medical and physical therapy appointments. Diane started to stay in bed late into the morning "because I can" and because "there really isn't anything else that I can do." Diane's husband and friends tried to encourage her to modify her activities by using a walker or crutches to get around, but she ignored these suggestions, insisting that she simply couldn't accept that her life had become so limited. She was angry and disillusioned and refused to accept the pain that she was experiencing, further exacerbating her distress. Her doctor suggested that she see a CBT therapist, and she reluctantly agreed. When we met for the first time, she said that her goals for therapy were to "make the pain go away" and to "fix her depression."

Don't Believe Everything You Think

We live in a world that emphasizes the importance of words and thoughts. This book you are now reading is an expression of how human beings rely on words and stories to describe and make meaning of things. Thoughts can be a powerful way for us to make sense of ourselves, others, and the world around us, but we sometimes forget that many of the thoughts we have are inaccurate and unhelpful. For instance, how many times have you had the thought "I can't do this," and then actually found you were able to do something? If we believed every thought that we had, we would be at the mercy of our brains, which generate hundreds of thoughts in reaction to the world around us. You may be having the thought "this book can't possibly help me," but the only way to know if that thought is true is to begin reading and practicing the skills outlined in the next few chapters.

Within the CBT model's three domains of change (thoughts, feelings, and behavior), thoughts are always the first place to begin when we are trying to improve depression symptoms and want to explore ways to feel better. Of course, thoughts don't exist independently of the other elements of the CBT model. Thoughts are generally related to our mood. For instance, we might look at our partner and think, "I am the luckiest person in the world to have found her to spend the rest of my life with," and feel a wave of love and joy. And in another situation, we might look at our partner and think, "How did I manage to marry the most irritating person in the world?" and feel frustrated and annoyed. Same partner, very different thoughts and feelings. We may even have these very different thought-feeling sequences in the span of five minutes, giving us a very good example of how these mood states and thoughts are fleeting and

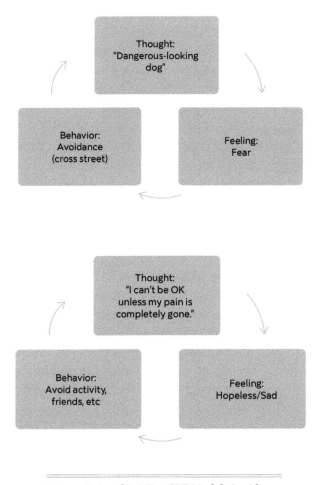

Figures 3.1 and 3.2 The CBT Model: Avoidance

mutable. But in the moment, we often believe our thoughts as if they are permanent facts rather than fleeting artifacts of our mood.

Identifying negative thinking and considering alternative thoughts that are more accurate and helpful is a critical skill in CBT treatment for depression. It seems like a very simple concept, but it can take time and practice to begin to notice our negative thoughts and how they are impacting our actions and moods. Once you have practiced the skill of noticing your negative thinking and balancing your thoughts, you will begin to notice that you feel better and behave in different ways that move you back toward the things in life that matter to you. Don't worry if practicing this skill feels awkward or overly simplistic. The skill is not asking you to "turn that frown upside down," it is asking you to become more aware of how your thoughts are impacting you and sustaining your depression.

I explained the elements of the CBT model to Diane and told her that we would begin by exploring how her thoughts were impacting her experience of her life. Diane was a little offended by this idea, saying, "It sounds like you're saying my thoughts aren't real. My thoughts are real, this pain is not acceptable, and I can't change the way I think about that." Diane was stuck in her negative thoughts about how her physical pain was responsible for her dissatisfaction and irritability. She believed that until the pain was 100 percent gone, she was not going to be able to engage in her life in a meaningful way. We spent a lot of time exploring how some of the thoughts she had about her life were impacting how she was feeling. As she became more aware of her thoughts and how they impacted her experience, she became more willing to consider alternative ways of thinking about her situation. Diane's physical pain was real, but how she responded and made sense of the pain with her thinking made a painful situation much worse.

These "stories" that our brains generate automatically are very powerful because often we are unaware of them and how they impact our experience and behavior. We believe them without evaluating their accuracy or helpfulness, leading us to respond in habitual ways that perpetuate more negative thinking. It can be difficult to learn the skill of noticing your thoughts before you choose your emotional and behavioral reactions. You may be walking down the street and see a large dog and automatically think "dangerous-looking dog" and cross the street. In these situations, the thought ("dangerous-looking dog"), feeling (fear), and action (avoidance) happen automatically, without examination.

In the example in figure 3.2, Diane really believed the thought, "I can't be okay unless my pain is completely gone," which led her to behave in ways that made her feel even more hopeless and unhappy, exacerbating her feelings of frustration and sadness and leading her to reject the suggestion that she could do less intense physical activities that may make her feel better. She spent most of her time at home thinking about her pain, or going to doctors trying to find solutions to her pain. This all-or-nothing thought left her trapped inside her mood (frustration and sadness), and believing this story made it impossible for her to consider alternative ways of looking at her situation.

DIANE was convinced that her injury was going to "ruin her retirement," and that there was "nothing left to look forward to" now that the kids were grown and her career was over. Every time her leg hurt or she noticed her limitations, she would make sense of it with these distorted thoughts about her injury and retirement. When I talked to her about the thinking errors that are common to depression, she got offended that I was implying that she "wasn't thinking clearly." As a retired teacher, she was certain that she had a very good brain. I explained that even supersmart people are vulnerable to these thinking errors when they are struggling with depression. She reluctantly reviewed a list of common thinking errors and noticed several that she used frequently. She could see that her all-or-nothing thinking about her injury was keeping her trapped and immobilized. She could also admit that she was "catastrophizing" when she said that her injury had "ruined her retirement." She had looked forward to retiring her whole life, assuming that she would love having no commitments. She was disappointed that her injury had interfered with her plans and left her feeling isolated and angry.

Distorted Thoughts

Now that we have established that our thoughts are not always helpful or accurate, we can begin to examine the unique ways that thoughts are distorted when we are depressed. Distorted thinking is the fuel that feeds the depression, maintaining inaccurate and negative beliefs about ourselves, others, and the world around us. Dr. Aaron Beck was a psychiatrist who noticed that his depressed patients had unusually high numbers of negative and inaccurate thoughts, and he proposed the theory that distorted thinking is an important feature of depression (Beck 1967).

Research has isolated several common thinking errors that we are vulnerable to when we are depressed (Beck 1976). It is helpful to recognize these common thinking patterns, in order to confirm when our thoughts are veering into the negative thought distortions common to depression. These thinking errors are something all of us engage in, but when we are depressed, we are even more likely to engage in these distorted thought patterns. Diane found that her thoughts fit the descriptions of "all-or-nothing thinking" and "catastrophizing." Knowing the common thinking errors can help you to recognize when you are falling into distorted thinking that may be impacting your mood and behavior. As you review this list, you are likely to recognize some thinking errors that feel very familiar to you.

Common Thinking Errors

COMMON THINKING ERRORS	EXAMPLES
All-or-nothing thinking – Seeing things in terms of absolutes or extremes. Things are either "perfect" or they are unacceptable.	"I have to please everyone or they will hate me." "I have to be the best or it is a total waste of time." "If I get a bad grade, I'm a total failure."
Black-and-white thinking – Ignoring the gray area. You know that you are using black-and-white thinking when you use the words "always" or "never."	"I will never be able to happy." "He is never there for me." "People always misunderstand me."
Catastrophizing – Drawing conclusions that predict worst-case scenarios or cataclysmic outcomes. This results in believing that the situation is hopeless and dire.	A person makes a mistake at work and assumes that they will be fired. "If I don't get this right, I will be ruined."
Discounting the positive – Devaluing positive information or feedback.	Someone gives you positive feedback, and you assume that they are "just being nice" or have some ulterior motive.

COMMON THINKING ERRORS	EXAMPLES
Personalization – Taking responsibility for events and situations that you are not actually responsible for.	Your employer is suddenly hit by a financial setback and you assume it is because you haven't been working hard enough. A friend doesn't return your text, so you conclude that she is upset with you.
Mistaking feelings for facts – Mistaking our feelings for reality.	The feeling of hopelessness becomes the belief that things are hopeless, or the feeling that we are unworthy becomes the belief that we are unworthy.
Overgeneralization – Generalizing that one experience means that another experience will have the same outcome.	Assuming that if therapy wasn't helpful in the past, then it will never be helpful, and thus overlooking that there are many types of therapy that might actually be more helpful.
Jumping to negative conclusions – Drawing negative conclusions in a situation when there is no evidence or indication to support that conclusion.	Deciding not to call a friend for support because "he wouldn't understand anyway." Your friend is late for a lunch date with you and you conclude that "he doesn't really want to see me."
Labeling – Creating simplistic labels for ourselves, others, and the world.	"I'm an idiot." "It's hopeless." "They are thoughtless."
Mind reading – Holding the fallacious belief that you know what others are thinking.	"I know what she's thinking." "I'm really good at reading faces..."
Focusing on the negative – Selectively paying attention to negative information in order to support negative thoughts and beliefs.	Focusing on the one negative comment on an otherwise fine job review. Fixating on the memories of awkward moments during an otherwise enjoyable dinner.
Emotional reasoning – Using feelings to draw what seem like logical conclusions.	"I feel hopeless, therefore it is hopeless." "I feel like a loser, therefore I am a loser."

Our brain is a highly efficient negative-thought-generating machine, but the good news is that we are starting to understand how this machine works. We know that negative thinking is the hallmark symptom of depression and that learning to notice and identify negative thoughts is the first step toward feeling better. Our emotional responses are directly related to our thinking, so if we can begin to become more aware of our thoughts, we can change our emotional reactions. The first step is to simply begin to become aware of thoughts as they arise. Thoughts are fleeting statements, evaluations, images, stories, and memories that are constantly being generated by our minds. Your brain is doing it right now. What are the automatic thoughts in your head at this moment?

Using Diane's story as an example, you can see that her rigid adherence to the story she told herself about her injury kept her trapped. We worked together to help her open up to alternative ways of looking at her life. Diane began to accept that the pain may be a part of her life indefinitely, but she could still participate in her life and do things that had meaning to her. She noticed that changing her thinking and moving back toward the things she cared about improved her mood and her experience of the pain.

The first step is to simply begin to intentionally notice thoughts as they arise. Pay particular attention to thoughts that link to strong negative feelings, because these are the thoughts that feed your

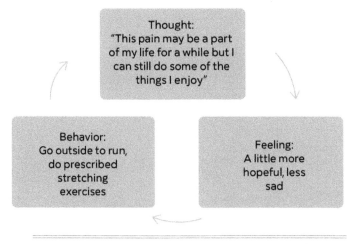

Figure 3.3 The CBT Model: Acceptance and changing thoughts

depression. The following strategies will help you begin to learn how to identify and record your negative thoughts.

Identify Your Negative Automatic Thoughts

Getting into the habit of recording your negative thoughts is a good way to begin to notice your thinking more. It also allows you to step back and consider how the thought is impacting the way you feel. CBT therapists use "thought records" to teach people how to record their automatic thoughts and begin to consider alternative ways of looking at situations. Our thoughts are generally attached to a feeling we are having as well. Beginning to notice these thoughts and connect them to a feeling is the first step in filling out a thought record.

Common Negative Thoughts Checklist

Take a look at the checklist of common negative thoughts. Are any of them familiar to you?

- ☐ Things always go wrong for me.
- ☐ No one will ever love me.
- ☐ People don't understand me.
- ☐ I will never be happy.
- ☐ I have to do everything right or I won't be loved.
- ☐ It's all on me.
- ☐ I never get an easy break.
- ☐ Life is harder for me.
- ☐ I'm not good enough.
- ☐ It's hopeless.
- ☐ Bad things are always happening to me.

Are there additional negative thoughts that come up for you often or that are coming up for you right now?

Now think about the feeling or mood you associate with each of these thoughts. The following list may help you identify your feelings:

- Depressed
- Sad
- Anxious
- Angry
- Ashamed
- Scared
- Loving
- Frustrated
- Disappointed
- Disgusted

- Content
- Enraged
- Grieving
- Grateful
- Happy
- Mad
- Panicked
- Agitated
- Excited

A simple way to start a thought record is to write in a journal whenever you are having a low or difficult mood, reflecting on the situation in which the mood occurred and what thoughts are associated with this feeling. This is the basis for identifying and changing our problematic thinking. We've provided a sample thought record in the appendix (see page 158), but you don't need to use a thought record to begin noticing and recording your thoughts and feelings. Simply use a journal to begin to record situations in which your thoughts and feelings are overly negative. We will review other steps toward examining and balancing our negative thoughts later in the chapter.

Why It Works: Identifying our negative automatic thoughts and connecting them to a feeling helps us become aware of the connection between how we think and how we feel, which is the first step in taking action to change.

SELENE was so excited to get into her first-choice college on the East Coast. When she got there, she was surprised to find that the workload and pace of the academics were more challenging than she had expected. She also hadn't expected to miss her family and friends on the West Coast as much as she did. Despite her long hours of studying, her grades were disappointing, and she was falling behind in several courses. She was overwhelmed and panicked, fearing that she might not be able to finish the semester. Thoughts that she wasn't smart enough and would never get caught up led her to feel even more hopeless. When a professor commented on one of her papers in class, saying that he thought that it was "excellent," she felt terrified rather than pleased. "Now he's going to notice me and expect excellent work from me. He's going to find out that paper was just a fluke and that I'm actually not that smart," she thought. She found herself sitting in the library for hours, lost in her negative thinking and not getting her work done. She started missing classes because she hadn't completed the assignments that were due. Her grades went down, which just fed her negative thought loop. She feared that she might fail out in her first semester of college.

Break Through Negative Thoughts

Once you've identified your problematic thoughts, it's time to find ways to combat them. Because these automatic thoughts are overly negative and distorted, we need to begin to examine the evidence that supports or contradicts them. When a judge in a courtroom sees that a case seems to be based mostly on "hearsay," she will interrupt the proceedings and ask, "Where's the evidence to support the case?" We will do just that with our negative thoughts, and see if there is evidence to support or challenge them. Then we can use the evidence we collect to come up with more accurate and balanced thoughts.

Researchers have found that people with depression have a "negative confirmation bias," which is the tendency to search for and favor information that supports our negative thoughts and beliefs (Oswald and Grosjean 2004). This tendency reinforces our negative beliefs and overlooks any evidence that might challenge the beliefs. This biased thinking can be counteracted by intentionally seeking evidence to disconfirm the negative thoughts.

An important step in combating negative thinking is to recognize when we are having particularly "charged thoughts." You may notice when you practice the next strategy that some thoughts are more intense, or charged, than others. You may also notice that these thoughts occur across different situations. We're going to pay special attention to these charged thoughts because they play a critical role in our depression.

Once we know the thoughts that are particularly charged for us, it is easier to notice when we are in a cycle of negative thinking. In the following strategy, you will notice that in Selene's example, the thoughts "I'm not smart enough" and "I'm going to fail" show up several times, and the corresponding feelings are scored very high. This gives us a clue that these are particularly charged thoughts for Selene, and play an important role in her depression. She can use this information to pay closer attention in situations that trigger these thoughts, and she can learn to combat this thinking with a more helpful interpretation of the situation.

Identify Your Thinking Errors

Being able to identify automatic thoughts allows us to examine them and consider how they may be impacting how we feel. One important way to recognize when our thoughts are distorted is to see if they fit one of the common thinking errors we reviewed earlier. We can expand on the thought record in the previous strategy to include the thinking errors associated with our thoughts and feelings. See the table on the next page for an example from Selene's story. Remember, this is something you're doing for yourself. No one's going to test you on this. Do the best you can and don't get stuck on "doing it right."

Looking over your thought records, are there any reoccurring thoughts that score particularly high for you? These are your charged thoughts and can provide special insight into your depression.

Why It Works: Practicing the skill of identifying automatic thoughts is a critical step toward managing your depression symptoms. The more you practice, the better you will get at identifying the thoughts linked to your mood, which is a key component in thought restructuring (a skill we will learn more about in chapters 5 and 8).

Selene's Negative Thoughts and Thinking Errors

SITUATION (WHO, WHAT, WHERE, WHEN, WHY?)	MOOD (IDENTIFY MOOD AND RATE INTENSITY FROM 1 TO 10)	NEGATIVE THOUGHT	THINKING ERROR (REFER TO THE LIST ON PAGES 34 TO 35)
Falling behind at school, grades falling	Disappointed (9) Panicked (8) Hopeless (9) Embarrassed (6)	I'm not smart enough. I'll never get caught up. I'm going to fail out of school. I'm going to look stupid.	Labeling Catastrophizing Catastrophizing
Teacher compliments paper in front of whole class	Embarrassed (4) Panicked (8) Ashamed (5) Hopeless (9)	He'll be watching even more closely. He'll find out I'm not smart enough. I'll look stupid. This is a fluke, I'm still going to fail.	Fortune-telling Fortune-telling Labeling Discounting

Put Negative Thoughts on Trial

Being able to identify automatic thoughts allows us to examine them and consider how they may be impacting how we feel. We often assume that these thoughts are "true." That is why it is important for us to put these thoughts "on trial" by considering the evidence that supports or disconfirms these negative thoughts. By doing this, we can restructure our thoughts, a core skill in CBT for depression.

Take one of the charged thoughts from your list in the previous exercise and consider the evidence that supports and disconfirms the thought. The example in the table on page 43 uses Selene's charged thought "I am going to fail" (rated 9 out of 10 in intensity).

Charged Thought: "I am going fail" (rated 9)

EVIDENCE IN SUPPORT OF THE THOUGHT	EVIDENCE AGAINST THE THOUGHT	CONSIDER THE EVIDENCE AND PROPOSE SOME ALTERNATIVE, MORE BALANCED THOUGHTS	WHAT ARE THE FEELINGS ASSOCIATED WITH THIS THOUGHT NOW AND WHAT IS THEIR INTENSITY? (0 TO 10)
I have gotten some bad grades on tests and papers. I have never had to work this hard at school.	I got the best grade on the paper in my history class. My grades have improved since the beginning of the semester. I am getting help from the academic center that may improve things. Therapy is helping me feel less hopeless.	It is going to be challenging, but I can probably make it through the semester with okay grades. I may not do as well as I did in high school, but I can pass most of my classes and move forward.	Anxious – 6 Relieved – 8 Hopeful – 7

Why It Works: When we find evidence against our automatic negative thoughts, we can prove to ourselves that the stories we tell ourselves aren't actually true, which can restructure our thinking and impact our feelings in powerful and positive ways.

Balance Fears and Predictions

Sometimes our negative automatic thoughts are fears or predictions that we are convinced will happen. Usually, we focus on the worst possible outcome, despite the fact that there are many other possible outcomes. Balancing our thinking by considering what lies between the extremes of the worst- and best-case scenarios allows us to refocus on more likely outcomes and flip negative thoughts to better reflect reality.

Think of a prediction or fear that you have been grappling with recently. This may have come up in an earlier exercise or be from a new situation.

The simple questions that follow are a way to unpack your fear-driven thoughts and move toward more probable predictions and expectations. The practice of stopping to consider the best, worst, and most probable outcomes can have a big impact on how you feel and behave in stressful situations.

1. What is the worst-case scenario?

2. What is the best-case scenario?

3. What is the most likely outcome? (Hint: Usually something between the best- and worst-case scenarios.)

4. If the worst-case scenario happened, what resources and support would you need?

5. Do you have access to some of those resources?

6. Now that you have answered these questions and considered other, alternative ways of looking at the situation, does that change how you are thinking and feeling about the situation?

Why It Works: Examining our fears and predictions and then finding practical solutions for them can help us see things more clearly and realistically. It can help alleviate the power that fear plays in our depression.

Key Takeaways

- Negative thinking is the hallmark symptom of depression. Learning to notice and identify negative thoughts is the first step toward feeling better.

- Our feelings generally arise from thoughts we are having about ourselves, others, and the world.

- When we become aware of our thoughts, the negative feelings that are a part of depression begin to make a lot more sense.

- The first step toward changing how you feel is beginning to identify the thoughts that underlie your mood.

- These thoughts are incredibly powerful mediators of our experience, yet when we examine them, they are often inaccurate and unhelpful.

- Distorted thinking is the fuel that feeds the depression and maintains inaccurate and negative beliefs about ourselves, others, and the world around us.

- Practicing the skill of identifying automatic thoughts and considering other, more balanced thoughts is a critical step toward managing your depression symptoms.

chapter 4

change your internal beliefs

Some people find that noticing, challenging, and changing their negative thinking is enough to help them feel better and move forward in their lives. Others find the thought restructuring helpful, but still find that certain negative thoughts are persistent and resistant to change. That is a clue that these really troublesome thoughts are linked to underlying internal beliefs that people are not really aware of. Internal beliefs are absolute statements about ourselves, others, the world, and the future, that we acquire in childhood and apply rigidly to all areas of our lives. We can work with these internal beliefs using skills that are very similar to the strategies for challenging distorted thoughts. Challenging and working to change these beliefs is another important strategy in CBT.

MAYAN'S family valued performance and achievement. Her parents rewarded her when she performed well and were disappointed if she experienced setbacks or failures. Her achievements were rewarded with praise and awards, while the inevitable failures and setbacks that every person experiences were considered catastrophic or embarrassing. Mayan had come to assume that she had to perform at her absolute best all of the time to be "good enough," and that all mistakes were unacceptable.

This belief had a huge impact on how Mayan approached high school and college. While her friends were spending a lot of their time socializing and doing fun things, Mayan put most of her attention on studying and doing schoolwork. She often overprepared for exams and presentations so there would be no risk that she would get a poor grade. She pushed herself to stay up late to study during final exams, and would return home exhausted and depleted. All of this effort yielded what she considered "good" results. She had good grades, but she really didn't know what she wanted out of life other than to "get good grades." She floundered after graduation because none of the jobs she was considered for seemed "important enough." It was hard for her to accept that all of her hard work led to an entry-level position doing menial tasks.

After a stressful job search, she took a job as a marketing assistant at a tech company. Everything was new to her and she felt overwhelmed. Her boss was very nice and supportive, but didn't give her very much direction, encouraging her to just "dive in and learn." She found this lack of structure and feedback on her performance difficult, and worried that she wasn't impressing her boss or coworkers. When her boss asked her to do a presentation at the next sales meeting, she spent weeks overpreparing. The day of the presentation, she was stressed and tense and forgot an important part of her presentation. She spent the evening berating herself and worrying that she was going to lose her job.

What Are Your Internal Beliefs?

In chapter 3, you learned how to identify your thoughts and determine how accurate and helpful they are in a given situation. If we apply those lessons to Mayan's story, we recognize that Mayan had thoughts that her presentation had to be perfect or she would disappoint her boss and lose her job. We have learned that once she is able to identify her perfectionist thinking, she will be able to consider alternative ways of looking at the situation that are more realistic and helpful.

While we know that thinking impacts how we feel and behave, if we dig a little deeper, we can begin to notice that these thoughts are informed by underlying beliefs and rules that we have about ourselves, the world, and other people. These internal beliefs are often learned from our families of origin, the communities that we belong to, or the broader cultural context we are raised in. Because they are woven so seamlessly into our lives and environments, we often mistake our beliefs for "reality" rather than another construction that we need to examine for accuracy and helpfulness.

In chapter 3, I encouraged you to not believe everything you think, and in this chapter, I am going to ask you not to believe everything you believe! Just like your thoughts, your internal beliefs are likely to be distorted and biased. Our internal beliefs are literally "at the root" of our thinking, and help to explain why it can be so difficult to challenge our automatic negative thoughts (Greenberger and Padesky, 2016). Nonetheless, we can become aware of these deeply rooted beliefs and begin to notice when they are feeding and supporting our negative thoughts. Because the root system of our internal beliefs is hardy and entrenched, it can be difficult to replace these beliefs with new internal beliefs.

Identifying our internal beliefs can be tricky because these beliefs "feel" so true and familiar to us. We have been living with these unexamined beliefs for much of our lives. Our internal beliefs are constructions or explanations that we developed in childhood to make sense of the people and world around us, and are the product of a natural survival mechanism. Children use black-and-white thinking to create rules that categorize their experiences as "good" or "bad," dangerous or safe. While we come by these beliefs honestly, when we carry them forward into our adult lives, they can become problematic. When Mayan's parents expressed disappointment every time she got a B rather than an A, or didn't get a gold medal at the swim meet, Mayan began to believe that her worth was contingent on her ability to perform above average on all tasks.

It makes perfect sense how the young Mayan would have come to these conclusions, but as an adult, she was left approaching adult life as if those rigid and simplistic childhood beliefs are still true. Somehow, we are able to leave Santa Claus behind in childhood, but not these maladaptive internal beliefs. One reason this may be true is that children are confronted with evidence to disconfirm the existence of Santa (Santa only eats Dad's favorite cookies, for instance), but not for these more entrenched internal beliefs that arc reinforced constantly by our families of origin, culture, and the world around us.

I like to think of internal beliefs as the "getaway car" that we construct during childhood to propel us through childhood and into adulthood. As adults, we don't need to fully abandon the getaway car, but we do want to stop and examine what it's constructed of, what we want to keep, and what we want to leave behind as we move forward in our lives. Mayan was able to recognize that the unrealistic and perfectionistic standards she held herself to were not helpful or even possible, but that she did want to maintain her belief in the importance of hard work and striving for excellence. This more pragmatic and mature internal belief will allow her to continue pursuing her goals with more realistic and compassionate expectations of herself.

One clue that can help us recognize when we are functioning based on internal beliefs is when we notice that we are making assumptions that are black and white, or all or nothing, such as "I will never be loved," or "People always let me down." These beliefs leave no room for alternatives or a more nuanced perspective. As you work toward recognizing your internal beliefs and how they impact your thinking, the ultimate goal is to be able to consider alternative beliefs that are more flexible and complex. If we can make space for other possibilities between these extremes, we can move toward more realistic beliefs about ourselves, other people, the world, and the future.

You can spot internal beliefs by recognizing these common features:

- Usually negative

- Absolute statements that are "all or nothing" or "black and white"

- Rigidly applied to most situations

- So deeply believed that we mistake them for "reality"

Common Internal Beliefs

Beliefs about the self:

I am unworthy.

I am worthless.

I'm unlovable.

I'm inadequate.

I'm unlikable.

I can't handle things.

I'm a screwup.

I will never be loved.

I am fragile or weak.

I must be beyond scrutiny to
be okay.

Beliefs about others:

People are cruel.

People are untrustworthy.

People are dangerous.

People will always let me down.

People are harsh and critical.

People are only out for themselves.

People don't like me.

People are more capable than I am.

People don't understand me.

Beliefs about the world:

The world is scary and dangerous.

The world works against me.

The world is harsh and punishing.

The world requires me to be perfect
all the time.

Beliefs about the Future:

The future is bleak.

The future is hopeless.

The future is scary.

Things are going to just get worse.

Identify Your Beliefs

One technique for identifying your internal beliefs is called the "downward arrow technique." This technique begins with the distorted thoughts we identified in chapter 3 and asks questions that allow you to go deeper into the internal beliefs that underlie these thoughts. Internal beliefs are often stated in language that is absolute and inflexible, and uses terms like "always" or "never."

We will use this technique to follow the thread from your automatic thoughts to your internal beliefs. For instance, in Mayan's case, her distorted thought was that if she didn't get her presentation completely perfect, her boss would be disappointed and fire her. The downward arrow technique demonstrated in the next section allowed her to reveal the underlying internal belief that fed this negative thinking.

Internal Beliefs about Myself:

"If this is true, what does it mean about me?"

SITUATION:
Mayan stays up all night making unnecessary changes to her presentation, trying to make it "perfect."

DISTORTED THOUGHT:
If this presentation isn't perfect, my boss will be disappointed and fire me.

If this is true, what does this mean about me?

I will only be good enough if I can always be perfect.

If this is true, what does this mean about me?

No matter how hard I try, I will never be good enough because I can't always be perfect.

If this is true, what does this mean about me?

I am not good enough.

Mayan was able to follow the arrow from a specific situation and thought to an absolute internal belief ("I am not good enough") that was at the core of her depression. Because she believed this internal belief without question, no matter how hard Mayan worked and progressed in her career, she always felt like she was falling short and "not good enough." The internal belief kept her trapped in this exhausting cycle of striving for perfection and inevitably falling short of this standard. Once Mayan was able to recognize this deeply internalized belief, she was able to assess how this belief was impacting the way she was approaching her life and work.

Internal Beliefs about Others:

"If this is true, what does it mean about others?"

Mayan also began to consider how this belief informed her beliefs about others. She was able to uncover internal beliefs about others as being overly harsh and critical. Her internal beliefs about others led her to thoughts that others were judging her harshly even when they may have been indifferent or impressed.

The downward arrow technique can be applied to her beliefs about others, too.

DISTORTED THOUGHT:
If this presentation isn't perfect, my boss will be disappointed and fire me.

If this is true, what does this mean about others?

Others expect perfection.

If this is true, what does this mean about others?

Others are harsh, critical, and unaccepting.

If this is true, what does this mean about others?

Others will reject me.

Internal Beliefs about the World:

"If this is true, what does it mean about the world?"

We can also use the downward arrow technique to follow the thread from our automatic thoughts to our internal beliefs about the world. Mayan was able to uncover internal beliefs about the world as being demanding and unreasonable. Her internal beliefs about the world as critical and unforgiving led to her thoughts that if she didn't get her presentation completely perfect, she would lose her job.

The downward arrow technique can be used to identify our internal beliefs of the world. Rather than asking what the thoughts tell us about ourselves or others, we ask what the thoughts mean about our view of the world.

DISTORTED THOUGHT:
If this presentation isn't perfect, my boss will be disappointed and fire me.

If this is true, what does this mean about the world?

The world expects perfection in all things.

If this is true, what does this mean about the world?

The world is demanding and unreasonable.

If this is true, what does this mean about the world?

The world is critical and unforgiving.

Why It Works: You can use this technique to begin to get a better understanding of the internal beliefs that underlie your problematic thinking. When we become aware of how these absolute and inflexible beliefs impact our view of the world and how it works, we can begin to question whether we want to allow them to dictate how we see the world.

Get Out of the If/Then Trap

Our internal beliefs are often expressed with if/then statements, which we then use to make predictions. This becomes problematic, because we then base our plans and actions on these predictions. These over-generalized "rules" often keep us from moving toward our goals and values in life.

Noticing when we are making if/then assumptions about situations provides another way of knowing when our thoughts are being colored by our distorted internal beliefs. For example, one of Mayan's if/then traps was the belief, "If I make a mistake, I am a failure." This if/then trap kept Mayan from trying new or challenging things or taking chances because she might make a mistake.

Common if/then traps include:

- ☐ If I can't be loved, then I cannot be happy.
- ☐ If I upset people, then they will reject me.
- ☐ If I disagree with people, then they will hurt me.
- ☐ If I make a mistake, then I am a failure.
- ☐ If I can't do something perfectly, then I shouldn't do it at all.
- ☐ If I let go of my exacting standards, then I will never do anything well.
- ☐ If someone is better than me at something, then it means that they are a better person.
- ☐ If I say something stupid, then people will think that I am stupid.
- ☐ If someone doesn't like me, then there is something wrong with me.
- ☐ If I ask for help, then people will know that I am weak.

☐ If I allow myself to feel my emotions, then I will completely lose control.

☐ If I let people help me, then I will completely lose my autonomy.

Notice if any of these feel familiar to you and reflect on whether you have any additional if/then traps to add to this list.

Why It Works: Falling into the if/then trap is part of being human. The fear center of the brain tries to reduce thinking to its most simplistic form. These simplistic rules become problematic when we believe them and choose to act in ways that limit us. Becoming aware of when we do this will help us make healthier decisions.

Change Your Beliefs

Much like negative automatic thoughts, once we've identified negative internal beliefs, CBT offers numerous tools to challenge and change them. Our internal beliefs are powerful because they are rigidly held and extreme beliefs about ourselves, others, the world, and the future. These beliefs limit us to simplistic all-or-nothing, if/then thinking that ignores the wider range of alternative outcomes. The strategies we will discuss in this section will enable you to consider alternative beliefs that are more complex and balanced, allowing a broader array of possible outcomes and expectations. Our old internal beliefs were formed when we were young and more simplistic thinking was understandable, but now that we are adults, we are capable of looking at things in a more flexible and nuanced way.

Our internal beliefs are like a small camera frame—we may be able to see a single tree through the limited frame, but not the whole forest. Questioning and reframing our internal beliefs allows us to shift from this limited view to a panoramic perspective that allows us to take in more of the details and specifics of the situation.

ADRIAN found challenging his thinking in most situations to be very helpful, but he noticed that this technique was not very helpful in situations related to his girlfriend and friends. He often felt fearful that she would see what a "loser" he was and break up with him. He couldn't seem to challenge his thoughts about being a failure who couldn't "get his act together." He withdrew from his girlfriend when he felt hurt or insecure, making him feel more alone and unloved. Despite the many things that his girlfriend did and said to show him that she loved him, Adrian only paid attention to the evidence that she didn't care about him. His irritability and sulkiness strained his relationship, and he did not share his thoughts or feelings with his girlfriend. She felt confused and shut out.

When he was feeling down, he stopped answering texts and calls from his friends, assuming that they didn't want to talk to him because he would just be "a downer." When his friends started calling less frequently, he used that as evidence to support his belief that people were unreliable and didn't really care about him. Adrian was unaware of how his internal beliefs were impacting how he was seeing his life and the decisions he was making.

When he learned about how his internal beliefs gave these thoughts more charge and impact, he uncovered several internal beliefs that were entrenched in his thinking. Adrian's parents divorced when he was five, and his father left the family, visiting infrequently. Adrian made sense of his father's departure as his fault, concluding that "he was unlovable" and that "people are unreliable." These internal beliefs made it very difficult for him to maintain friendships and romantic relationships, which he valued very deeply. These beliefs colored his thinking about relationships, others, and the world in ways that reinforced these beliefs. He had several relationships that failed, and he used those experiences to support his beliefs about himself and others. Adrian learned that his internal beliefs included "I will never find someone who really loves me," and "People always leave eventually." Once he became aware of the beliefs underlying his negative thoughts, he could consider alternative beliefs that allowed him to see other perspectives.

As mentioned in chapter 3, research has found that one of the most effective ways to combat our dysfunctional thoughts and beliefs is to approach them like a scientist or a judge and ask. "Where is the evidence to confirm or disconfirm this belief?" and "Is there a way to test this belief?" When you recognize these rigid rules and understand the evidence for and against them, you can begin to consider more complex and nuanced ways to view the situation that will allow you to move forward with more realistic expectations.

Challenge Internal Beliefs with Evidence

Pick one internal belief or if/then trap that is impacting your current life and functioning. Work through the questions in Adrian's example below.

Internal Belief to be challenged:

Adrian: *I will never find someone who really loves me.*

How much do you believe this internal belief? (0 means not at all and 10 means completely)

Adrian: *9*

List any evidence and experiences that demonstrate that this belief is not *always* true *all* of the time:

Adrian:

1. *My girlfriend tells me almost every day that she really loves me.*
2. *My girlfriend plans romantic things to do and leaves me notes in the morning to remind me that she cares.*
3. *My mom and grandparents really love me.*

4. *I had a girlfriend in high school who really seemed to care about me.*

5. *I was really close to my roommate in college and he has stayed in touch over the years.*

6. *I've dated quite a few people and some of them seemed to want to get to know me better.*

Review the evidence and experiences that contradict your internal belief. How does this evidence change how much you believe this internal belief?

Adrian: *When I really think about it, most of my relationships have ended because I didn't believe that the person really cared, not because they didn't say that they cared. I think this belief seemed more like a fact to me before, like "Of course she doesn't love me, why even try?" Now I realize that may not be true, like maybe she does care, but it's hard for me to believe it because this other belief gets in the way. Challenging this belief is going to help me hear it when my girlfriend tells me how much I mean to her.*

How much do you believe this internal belief now? (0 means not at all and 10 means completely)

Adrian: *5*

Can you think of more accurate and balanced internal beliefs based on this evidence? Put a number next to each of these new beliefs that measures how much you believe each one. (0 means not at all and 10 means completely)

Adrian:

Not everyone loves me, but some people do. 7

I am loveable sometimes. 8
Some people actually really do care about me, it is just hard for me to take that in. 8

Why It Works: Our brains have evolved to keep us safe, and naturally try to reduce our thinking to simple, all-or-nothing rules. By identifying our old internal beliefs and considering more accurate and helpful beliefs, we are literally retraining our brain to evaluate the world in more complex, relevant, and nuanced terms.

Challenge Internal Beliefs and Rules with Experiments

Sometimes life gives us opportunities to test our rules and beliefs without conducting an actual experiment. For example, Mayan believed that if she didn't do the presentation perfectly, her boss would fire her. When she finally presented her work at the meeting, she made a few mistakes, but her boss didn't fire her. In fact, he complimented her on several parts of the presentation and made some suggestions about how she could improve it for next time. This was a real-life situation that Mayan could use as an opportunity to collect evidence to disconfirm her internal belief.

We can also construct actual experiments to test the validity of the rules we construct based on our beliefs. This is called a behavioral experiment, and it is a core skill used in CBT. This is how to conduct a behavioral experiment to test an internal belief.

Step 1: Identify a rule from the if/then trap exercise or a belief you want to test.

Adrian: If I tell my girlfriend when I am feeling insecure about our relationship, then she will look down on me or want to break up with me.

How much do you believe this internal belief right now? (0 means not at all and 10 means completely)

Adrian: 7

Step 2: Think of behaviors that would allow you to test the validity of this belief.

Adrian: *When I feel insecure about our relationship, I can tell my girl-friend how I am feeling and ask her if she feels differently about me after I have shared with her.*

Step 3: What do you expect will happen when you do the behavior from step 2?

Adrian: *She might be understanding at first, but will get tired of hearing about my insecurities about the relationship.*

Step 4: Perform the experiment by doing the task and collecting data about the experience

Adrian:

- *Time 1: She told me she loved me and wanted to know when I was feeling insecure. We had a really nice afternoon.*
- *Time 2: She was really surprised that I thought she wanted to break up with me. She told me that she was committed to our relationship.*
- *Time 3: She asked me to tell her when I was having these feelings so she could reassure me and help me feel better.*

Step 5: Compare your predictions to the results.

Adrian: *It was really hard to do at first, and I was surprised by my girl-friend's reaction, but it made me feel closer to her and has improved our communication. I feel more confident now that I have proof that reality doesn't match my fears and expectations.*

Why It Works: We have talked about ways the brain tries to oversim-plify things to create rigid, easily applied rules to predict outcomes, but luckily our brains are also built to process information in more complex and helpful ways. Collecting evidence to support or disconfirm our thoughts and beliefs is one of the ways humans are able to challenge rigid thoughts and beliefs and support more complex and nuanced perspectives.

Key Takeaways

- Thoughts are informed by underlying beliefs that we have about ourselves, the world, and other people.

- Our internal belief system is like the root system underlying the plant that produces the many distorted thoughts that maintain depression.

- Because our internal beliefs are woven so seamlessly into our lives and environments, we often mistake our beliefs for reality, rather than another construction that we need to examine for accuracy and helpfulness.

- One clue that can help us recognize when we are functioning based on internal beliefs is when we notice that we are making assumptions that are black and white, or all or nothing, such as, "I will never be loved," or "People always let me down."

- Our goal is to be able to consider alternative beliefs that are more flexible and complex.

- We can use the downward arrow technique to follow the thread from our automatic negative thoughts to our internal beliefs.

- Sometimes we turn our internal beliefs into rigid rules that we use to create predictions.

- Collecting evidence to support or disconfirm our thoughts and beliefs is one of the ways we are able to challenge rigid thoughts and beliefs and support more complex and nuanced perspectives.

Part Three

Connect with Your Feelings

We have spent the past few chapters talking about thoughts and beliefs that impact depression, but most of you probably picked up this book because of how you feel. The reason most people seek out psychological treatment is because they want to get rid of unwanted, distressing feelings. When we are depressed, we often experience emotions such as sadness, hopelessness, irritability, guilt, and shame, which can be so intense they feel debilitating. This section will provide key CBT skills and strategies for managing emotional experiences like these. We will also go over some helpful mindfulness techniques that are essential for emotional regulation and cultivating an internal sense of peace.

chapter 5

deal with your emotions

Negative feelings are an inescapable part of the human experience and at the core of our struggle with depression, but there are ways to stop wrestling with our emotions and begin to relate to them in a healthier way. This chapter will focus on three CBT proficiencies in working with our emotions: number one is the ability to identify our emotions in clear and precise terms, number two involves learning how our emotions impact our thinking and behaviors, and number three enables us to distinguish between reacting and responding to emotional experiences. We can't get rid of emotions, but we can learn concepts, skills, and strategies that will enable us to relate to our emotions in a different way.

ADIA had known that she wanted to be a mother for as long as she could remember. She loved children and had grown up in a large family. She hadn't anticipated that she would find staying home with her new baby to be so difficult and exhausting. She felt depleted and overwhelmed by the constant feeding and care that the baby needed, and she was ashamed that she was finding that time in her life so difficult. Her mother and sisters had assured her that having a baby would be the "best experience she could ever have," but she had never felt so overwhelmed and unable to cope. Her husband had to return to work after two weeks, leaving her feeling even more tired and isolated. She resented that he could go to work while she had to stay at home to care for their new daughter. She was irritable and angry when her husband got home, and rebuked his efforts to get her to go out with friends or take a nap. She cried when he would leave for work, feeling alone and desperate for some relief.

Emotions 101

Emotions color every moment of our lives. From the moment we wake up, we respond to our lives emotionally. We might wake up and feel happy to see that the sun is shining, or worried because we remember the important presentation we are giving later in the day. Notice that our emotions are defined by our thoughts and the situation that we are in. And these emotions impact what we do with these thoughts and situations. We might snuggle back into our covers with a smile and enjoy a few more minutes in bed if we are feeling happy and contented, or leap quickly out of bed and dash for the shower if we are worried about an unfinished project at work. Emotions inform our choices and motivate us to act. Despite the critical role that emotions play in our lives, most of us spend a lot of our time trying not to experience our emotions. In fact, I would guess that one of the reasons you picked up this book is your desire not to feel what you are currently feeling.

The most common reason that people show up in my therapy office is that they don't want to feel the way that they are feeling. Who wouldn't want to be free of emotions like sadness, hopelessness, helplessness, irritability, anger, guilt, fearfulness, and despair? These are not emotions any of us want to have, but these are emotions that all of us will experience in the course of our lives. Because we identify these emotions as "negative," we respond to them like any other adverse thing and try to avoid them. Sadly, this ends up having the opposite effect. Avoidance only increases the intensity of our negative emotional experience, leading to a vicious cycle that is hard to get out of.

Our brains have evolved to avoid things it recognizes as "dangerous" or unpleasant. Our natural defense system allows for three possible reactions to a dangerous situation: fight, flight, or freeze. This has enabled animals and humans to evolve and thrive in a dangerous world.

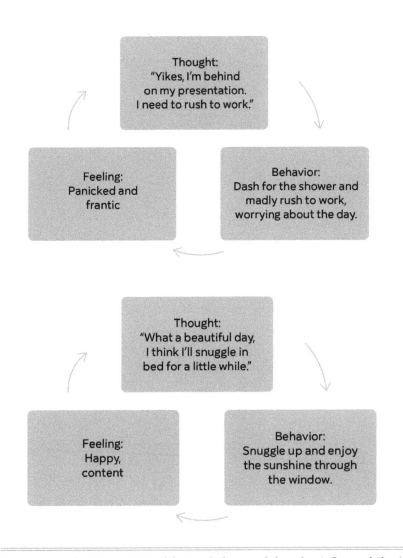

Figures 5.1 and 5.2 The CBT Model: How feelings and thoughts influence behavior

When a rabbit sees a fox, it will run (flight); if outpaced, it will simply flop over and "play dead" (freeze); or, if the assailant isn't too scary, the rabbit may choose to fight. When humans were living in a world where real physical danger was a part of day-to-day life, this fear system was an effective way to enable them to survive. In our current lives, we are rarely faced with grave danger of, say, a grizzly bear, but we still have a brain that is wired to respond to "danger" with the same fight, flight, or freeze response. This becomes problematic when we respond to social and emotional "threats" with our survival instincts. It makes perfect sense that we would want to avoid a predator by running and hiding, but what if we have the same response with our experiences of emotional danger? There are many ways that we try to avoid emotional "danger" or pain. We might use drugs or alcohol, or we may avoid new social situations or taking risks in relationships. These avoidance strategies may take away the discomfort in the short term, but they make the problem worse over time.

Understanding our fear system and how it increases our tendency to avoid adverse experiences helps us understand how we come by avoidance naturally. We don't avoid negative emotional experiences because we are weak, but because we are wired to do so. Avoidance is still helpful in some situations. Opening an umbrella when it rains is an effective use of avoidance. Not answering phone calls from your boss because you are worried that he is angry with you is not an effective use of avoidance.

CBT helps us learn how to avoid avoidance and walk toward the discomfort that life naturally delivers to all of us. Learning to recognize when our brains are responding to discomfort as danger helps us begin to relate to our emotions in a different way. Discomfort is a part of all of our lives. In fact, it is often a measure of a rich and full life, because when we are challenging ourselves and pursuing things that matter to us, it is inevitable that we will experience stress and challenges. Learning to accept this discomfort and relate to it as a part of living a meaningful life is an important step toward changing how you relate to your emotions.

Skill number one in our Emotions 101 curriculum is learning to identify and name our emotions. This may be harder than you think. Often, we categorize emotions as simply "bad" or "good." It is natural that we want to have more of the "good" ones and less of the "bad" ones. Nonetheless, there are literally hundreds of words to describe our emotional experience. When we can gain access to a broader emotional vocabulary, we can move beyond this black-and-white experience of our feelings. We can learn to access the richness and complexity of our emotional world while not letting it drive our behaviors or experience (Prinze, 2004; Storm and Storm, 1987).

Recent research on emotions has found that if we are able to identify and name our emotions, we are able to change the way that we experience these emotions. This research has also found that through improving our emotional vocabulary, or increasing the number of words we have to describe the broad array of emotions that we experience, we can improve our ability to respond to emotions more flexibly. Take a look at the list of emotions in the Vocabulary of Emotions/Feelings chart later in this chapter (page 75). Research has identified the core emotions that are expressed and experienced by most human beings on the top line of the chart. More recent research has found that when people are able to consider and label their emotions with even more precise terms (listed in the chart), they are able to regulate and respond to their emotions more effectively.

Skill number two is learning how these emotions impact our experience, behavior, and thinking. By unpacking the emotions and linking them to her situation and negative thinking, Adia was able to begin to behave in ways that allowed her to change the situation. For instance, she asked her sister if she could come over more often to help with the baby, and she joined a new mothers' group to get support from other moms who were going through the same thing.

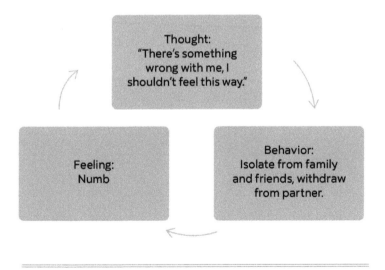

Figure 5.3 The CBT Model: Negative thoughts-behavior-feelings cycle

WHEN Adia finally showed up in my office, she couldn't describe how she was feeling. She would sit in the chair and cry quietly and say that she simply felt "numb" or "nothing at all." When I shared that sometimes numbness is an attempt to avoid feeling what we are feeling, she shrugged and slumped back in her chair. With time, Adia was able to look deeper and recognize the emotions being generated by the challenges she was facing. Adia was able to identify that the core emotions she was feeling as a new mother to a fussy infant were sadness, stress, and anger. When she dug even deeper, she was able to recognize her feelings of hurt and loneliness, as well as guilt (for having these feelings, because others had told her that this "should be the most wonderful time in her life"). She also felt irritated, resentful, and even a little jealous that her partner was away at work all day while she stayed at home to care for their baby. Adia's initial response to her negative emotions was to avoid them by suppressing and numbing them. Once she was able to recognize that this response was actually worsening her experience, she could begin to consider other ways to respond to her experience, including seeking out advice from a therapist and her sisters and taking time for herself when her husband got home from work.

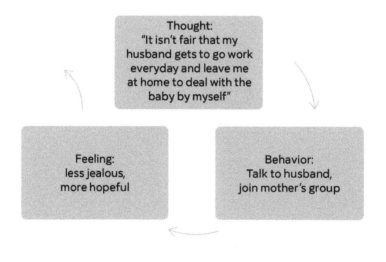

Figure 5.4 The CBT Model: Breaking the cycle with changing behavior

Get in Touch with Your Emotions

Many of you chose to read this book because there are emotions that you simply do not want to have. While completely understandable, there isn't a book or expert that can tell you how to eliminate negative emotions from your experience. Our attempts to avoid intense emotions can get in the way of our ability to live our lives. Learning to recognize and relate to your emotions as an unavoidable part of a meaningful life will allow you to move forward even when you are experiencing intense or difficult emotions.

We spend a lot of our time and energy trying to avoid negative emotions and maintain positive emotions. These attempts to control our emotional experience are often at the root of our depression. Research on emotional regulation has isolated many of the strategies that we use to try to control or change our emotional experience. Often these strategies require us to choose between reacting and responding. When we experience an adverse or uncomfortable emotion, our evolutionarily hardwired reaction is to avoid this emotion. A more adaptive "response" is likely to involve a conscious choice to "approach" the experience.

Adia's initial response to her negative emotions was to avoid them by suppressing and numbing them. Once she was able to recognize that this response was actually worsening her experience, she could begin to consider other ways to respond to her experience, including seeking out advice from a therapist and taking time for herself when her husband got home from work. Adia was able to switch from avoidance behaviors to approach behaviors, a key skill for managing depression.

Skill number three is learning to shift from reacting to responding to our emotional experiences. When we impulsively act on the urge connected to an emotion without pausing or considering alternative responses, we are reacting. Acting as if these urges are the unavoidable outcome to emotional experiences gets us caught in a cycle of reacting. When we are angry, we lash out; when we are sad, we withdraw; when we feel powerless, we give up. This is linked to the fear system that we discussed earlier, the one that evolved to keep us physically safe in a dangerous world. Reacting to the experience of being very cold by putting on a jacket or lighting a fire is an adaptive response, but not when we apply these simplistic rules to our emotional experience. Reacting to adverse emotional experiences with emotional avoidance strategies such as drinking alcohol or isolating ourselves from our social networks is not a functional application of avoidance. That is why we must learn to recognize that while our brain may be hardwired to react, we are able to be aware of the "urge" without acting on that urge. When we can do this, we are able to consider alternative responses. Rather than reacting immediately and habitually, without thinking, responding requires us to pause so we can make a conscious choice about how we want to move forward.

ADIA had a hard time recognizing her emotions and using them to understand what she needed. Once she was able to label her emotions more precisely, she was able to communicate with her husband to tell him what she needed. This didn't happen right away, and she had to learn that when she reacted to the urges that her emotions supplied, she often behaved in ways that made things worse. When her husband came home from work, she would often be tired and irritable. When he didn't immediately pick up the baby and ask Adia what she needed, she would react by withdrawing from him to stew alone. This made him feel confused and frustrated, so he would often just leave her alone—exactly what she didn't want! She had to learn to stop and pause to check in with herself so she could respond in a more effective way, like asking him to take the baby for an hour so she could take a nap or exercise.

Label Your Emotions

Some individuals have difficulty pinpointing the emotions they have. This strategy will help you put a name to your feelings and identify how they are affecting your life. Because we know that feelings are the consequence of the situation we are in and/or the thoughts we are having about the situation, identifying the situation and thoughts can help us explore or emotions.

Identify a situation in which you were feeling particularly depressed or down, and find the appropriate feelings in the Vocabulary of Emotions/Feelings chart (Drummond, 2020). The more specific you can be about your feelings, the better.

Vocabulary of Emotions/Feelings

CORE EMOTIONS	MORE PRECISE EMOTIONS
Happy	Contented, Optimistic, Glad, Gratified, Pleased, Satisfied, Serene, Sunny, Enthralled, Aglow, Buoyant, Cheerful, Hopeful, Proud, Gleeful, Lighthearted, Upbeat, Blissful, Excited, Delighted
Sad	Neglected, Incomplete, Ashamed, Despairing, Morose, Weak, Unhappy, Disappointed, Gloomy, Worried, Alienated, Broken, Powerless, Hopeless, Damaged, Empty, Defeated, Regretful, Guilty, Lonely
Love	Adoring, Desiring, Attached, Tender, Cherishing, Compassionate, Devoted, Doting, Affectionate, Admiring, Longing, Idolizing, Infatuated, Passionate, Attracted, Trusting, Secure, Satisfied, Romantic, Sentimental, Euphoric
Angry	Irritated, Cranky, Impatient, Heated, Resentful, Sullen, Uptight, Crabby, Offended, Disgusted, Belligerent, Envious, Enraged, Grouchy, Jealous, Furious, Seething, Vindictive
Surprise	Stunned, Amazed, Moved, Overcome, Confused, Touched, Astonished, Awed, Impressed, Astounded, Excited
Fear	Nervous, Tense, Uneasy, Scared, Insecure, Cautious, Hesitant, Avoidant, Shy, Timid, Watchful, Worried, Alarmed, Apprehensive, Defensive, Fidgety, Panicked, Skittish, Threatened

Here is an example of Adia completing this exercise:

SITUATION	CORE EMOTIONS (CHOOSE FROM THE LEFT COLUMN OF THE CHART)	MORE PRECISE EMOTIONS (CHOOSE FROM THE RIGHT COLUMN OF THE CHART)
Adia: My husband leaves for work and I and I am left alone to deal with the baby	Fear, Surprise, Love	Resentful, Abandoned , Doting (John and Gross, 2004)

Why It Works: Recent research has shown that if we are able to label our emotions in more complex and precise terms, we can regulate these emotions more effectively. Increasing and using a more precise emotional vocabulary shifts our brains from the simplistic, black-and-white expressions of emotions like good and bad or sad and happy, and enables us to have a more nuanced response.

Emotional Regulation Strategies

Researchers have identified four main strategies that enhance our ability to regulate our emotional responses in distressing situations, which we can remember with the acronym TANS:

Thought restructuring

Acceptance

Normalizing

Self-compassion

These strategies allow us to approach uncomfortable feelings rather than avoid them.

Consider walking through the following list of emotion regulation strategies and questions whenever you are struggling with difficult experiences to see if they allow you to navigate the experience in a different way.

Thought Restructuring: Thought restructuring is very similar to the strategies we practiced in chapters 4 and 5, when we acquired evidence to challenge our automatic negative thoughts and internal beliefs. If we are able to step back from a situation and consider how accurate and helpful our thinking is about it, we are likely to change how we feel about the situation.

» **Questions to consider:** Are the thoughts that you were having about the situation accurate or helpful? Are there alternative ways of looking at the situation that may have been more accurate or helpful?

Acceptance: Acceptance is the opposite of avoidance. Our brains are hardwired to react to adverse experiences with avoidance. Acceptance means that we choose to do the opposite, and make space for the experience as it is. By doing this, we are able to be informed by the emotion and what it may be telling us. Acceptance also allows us to learn that we can tolerate our emotional experiences, no matter how painful they may be. When we resist and avoid our emotional experiences, we often make those feelings last longer and persist more intensely. The things we resist will persist. People sometimes mistake acceptance with resignation or choosing to refrain from actions to remedy the situation, but acceptance means that you accept the situation or experience for what it is right now as you move through it.

» **Questions to consider:** What would be different if you could accept the experience and the emotions you are having? If you could make space for the emotions and experience, could you move forward in a different way?

Normalizing: Normalizing involves recognizing that difficult emotions and experiences are part of the human experience. All of us experience loss, failure, frustration, and setbacks, not because we are weak, but because we are human. It is impossible to avoid these things if we are living, working, and pursuing our goals or interests.

» **Questions to consider:** Is this experience something that could only happen to you, or is this something that happens to most people at some time? For instance, if the experience was being turned down when you asked someone out on a date, do you think this is likely to happen to most people? How does this change the way you feel about the situation? →

Self-compassion: Self-compassion is one of the most difficult concepts to promote to people who are experiencing depression. When we are depressed, we are often very self-critical. We have thoughts that we are weak, lazy, unlovable, and so on. We blame ourselves for our depression and assume that it is our fault. Self-compassion requires us to view ourselves and our situation with the gentle, nonjudgmental eyes of a trusted friend.

» **Questions to consider:** Did you criticize or judge yourself for this situation? What would you say to a friend in a similar situation? Why is it hard to say these kind things to yourself? What might have been different if you had been able to say something calming and encouraging to yourself at the time?

How Do Your Emotions Affect Your Life?

We have explored why we have emotions, how being aware of the common reactions to emotions can help us choose to respond in healthier ways, and how our attempts to control and avoid them often make our depression worse. In this exercise, we are going to apply these concepts in our daily life. Over the next few days, notice situations that trigger particularly intense emotions and then walk through the questions outlined in Adia's example. This will help you learn more about what emotions are particularly sticky for you and how you react to these sticky emotions. It will also help you consider alternative responses that you can choose next time you find yourself in a similar situation.

SITUATION:

Adia: My husband gets home from work and doesn't ask me if he can take the baby for a while so I can rest.

Emotion(s):

Angry, frustrated, hurt, overwhelmed

Urge:

Yell at him and tell him he's incredibly selfish.
I want to: Avoid, Withdraw, Isolate, Reject, Push away, Hide, Give up,
Not act, Attack

Actual Response:

Adia: *I didn't yell at him because I didn't want to upset the baby. I banged around in the kitchen and wouldn't talk to him when he asked me what was wrong. He got mad and just left to watch TV, which made me feel even more upset and lonely.*

Was this an example of approach or avoidance behavior?

Adia: *Avoidance. It did make me feel worse in the end. We made up later, but it ruined our night because I couldn't just ask for what I needed.*

Did you use any of the four TANS (Thought restructuring, Acceptance, Normalizing, Self-compassion) emotional regulation strategies?

Adia: *No.*

If you could redo it, is there anything you would do differently in this situation? What would have been different if you had been able to use any of the TANS emotional regulation strategies?

Adia: *I would have tried to recognize how I was feeling and tell my husband what I needed when he got home (rather than expecting him to just know what I needed).*

Why It Works: Becoming aware of our urges and reactions to difficult emotions, and the consequences of following through on them, helps us recognize when we need to pause and use our emotional regulation strategies to help us respond in a more skillful way.

STOP Letting Emotional Reactions Drive Your Behavior

STOP is a strategy that helps you respond rather than react to a difficult emotional experience. This simple practice allows you to pause, take a breath, and observe the situation and what you are feeling before you proceed with your more measured response (Drucker 1954).

S – Stop rather than react

T – Take a breath

O – Observe the situation as it is without judgment

P – Proceed with a response you choose

Can you think about a situation in which you reacted rather than responded? Maybe it was on your drive to work when you honked your horn and yelled at the person that cut in front of you at the tollbooth. What might have been different if you had used the STOP technique? Maybe you would have stopped, taken a breath, noticed that the person was actually human just like you and anxious to get to work, or maybe having a bad day, and rather than honking simply allowed them to enter your lane to the tollbooth.

Think back to something that happened recently or in your past that caused you significant distress, or a situation in which you reacted to the experience in an intense or negative way. Maybe a moment when you snapped at a loved one or overreacted to a situation.

What was the situation?
(who, what, where, when)

How did you respond?
Was this an avoidance response?

How did the experience turn out?

What might have been different if you had used the STOP technique before your reaction?

S – Stop rather than react

T – Take a breath

O – Observe the situation as it is without judgment

P – Proceed with a response you choose

What would responding rather than reacting change about these kinds of situations?

Try to use the STOP technique in your daily life. It can be helpful to notice the clues that might let you know that you are about to react rather than respond to a situation. Some people notice that when they are in a reactive state, their heart races, or they clench their jaw, or their face flushes. Try to notice when you are getting clues that you are in a situation where you could choose to STOP rather than react in ways that you may regret later. The more we practice these skills, the more they start to become second nature.

Why It Works: There are many reasons why this practice works so well. Research shows that when we step back from a situation for just a few seconds, we are able to broaden our perspectives and proceed with greater clarity. Taking a breath allows our minds and bodies to shift from reaction mode to a calmer state that will allow us to respond rather than react.

Key Takeaways

- The reason most people seek out psychological help or treatment is because they want to get rid of unwanted, distressing feelings.

- When we are depressed, we often experience emotions such as sadness, hopelessness, irritability, guilt, and shame.

- We spend a lot of our time and energy trying to avoid negative emotions and maintain positive emotions. These attempts to control our emotional experiences are often at the root of our depression.

- Avoidance only increases the intensity of our negative emotional experiences, leading to a vicious cycle that is hard to get out of.

- When we experience an adverse or uncomfortable emotion, our evolutionarily hardwired reaction is to avoid this emotion, while a more adaptive response is likely to involve a conscious choice to approach the experience.

- Only by intentionally choosing to experience negative emotions can we learn that we are able to tolerate them far better than we think we can.

- Practicing the four emotional regulation strategies can help us shift from reacting to responding.

chapter 6

be mindful

Mindfulness is a state of being that is natural to all humans, but one that modern life makes increasingly difficult to access. Can you think of the last time you were fully present in a moment, when you were neither ruminating about the past or worrying about the future? This is the basis of mindfulness. This chapter will walk you through several exercises that will allow you to experience moments of mindfulness, and encourage you to practice these as a part of your efforts to move through your depression.

DILIP was a committed husband, father, and pediatrician who worked very hard to meet the many demands of his busy life. He loved his family and job, and couldn't understand why he never felt "happy" or content with his life and accomplishments. At the end of the day, he would lie in bed thinking of the things he didn't get done and what he needed to do the following day. His self-esteem was contingent on fulfilling all of these roles flawlessly all of the time. When something inevitably went wrong, he would berate himself relentlessly for his "stupid mistakes" and thoughtlessness. All of his time, energy, and attention was spent caring for others and avoiding mistakes, leaving little time to be present with his loved ones or to consider what all of this "doing" was about.

Stay Present

Mindfulness has become a buzzword in our culture, but what does it really mean? I have noticed in my work that people often respond to the word "mindfulness" with the same resistance and judgment these practices target. They will roll their eyes and comment that they aren't into that "woo woo" stuff, or that it's boring, or that they don't have time because they have more important things to do. I often hear that they have tried to meditate, but that it didn't help or they were "bad at it." Do any of these ring true for you? Are there other reasons you might be resistant to trying a mindfulness practice?

Sometimes people are caught off guard when I teach mindfulness practices as a part of CBT treatments for depression, because they think CBT is a scientifically validated treatment (it is). They are surprised to learn that there is a growing body of empirical evidence that supports the use of mindfulness techniques to improve psychological flexibility and emotion regulation. Mindfulness practices have been found to significantly improve depression, anxiety, insomnia, and general life satisfaction.

There is nothing "woo woo" about basic mindfulness practice. It is simply a call to "be here now." Mindfulness practices teach us how to focus our awareness on the present moment, with kindness and curiosity, and without judgment. They help us cultivate the ability to stay in our experience as it is, rather than be trapped in our minds, struggling with the way we want (or don't want) it to be. Mindfulness practices ask us to sit with our experience as it unfolds, whether the moment is difficult or pleasurable or tedious. These skills allow us to build our repertoire of ways to relate to our emotional world flexibly and compassionately. The term "mindfulness" in this sense is relatively new, but it refers to practices and ideas from ancient philosophies and religions, including Buddhism and stoicism. Mindfulness offers us a path toward living our lives with more presence and purpose.

Mindfulness is an important part of current CBT treatment protocols such as MBCT (mindfulness-based cognitive therapy). MBCT was developed by Dr. J. Teasdale and his colleagues as a treatment specifically for chronic depression. The treatment combines mindfulness practices with standard CBT concepts such as psychoeducation, cognitive restructuring, and behavioral experiments. While many of these practices would be considered "new" to CBT, traditional CBT has always emphasized the use of techniques that would allow individuals to attend to and track their experiences, thoughts, and behaviors, and consider alternative perspectives.

MBCT proposes that moving from making meaning about our experience to simply being in the experience has a profound impact on how we relate to that experience. This is true for how we choose to relate to our emotions and thoughts and beliefs. Mindful awareness and acceptance require us to recognize that we often add a layer of meaning to our experiences that actually distorts and intensifies the experience. Buddhism has long had an understanding of this concept: **Suffering = Pain x Resistance**. In other words, pain is the unavoidable consequence of being alive, but the suffering that we experience is exponential to our level of resistance. If we can accept and allow the pain and discomfort that a meaningful life inevitably delivers, we are able to move through, endure, and maybe even grow from the experience (Kuyken, Watkins, Holden, et al. 2010).

When we judge, resist, react to, and wrestle with not wanting to have our emotions, we transform the unavoidable pain that life delivers into a more intense and prolonged experience of suffering. For instance, we can touch, taste, smell, and see an anchovy with curiosity and nonjudgment and notice that it is soft, salty, acrid, and gray/black, or we can experience it with a judgmental eye, and it becomes an unappealing, mushy, foul-smelling, gross-tasting, gray/black atrocity! The first stance observes, describes, and allows the experience to be simply what it is, while the second stance engages us in judging and resisting the experience because we have added the layer of meaning, or the story, that anchovies are disgusting, foul, and unpalatable.

We create more suffering for ourselves through our efforts to avoid or change the experience rather than just allowing it to be what it is. These efforts generally result in more and prolonged experiences of emotional discomfort. When we are able to be present in the reality of our life as it is, we can allow the events and emotions that occur to be as they are, and to still move forward in our lives. It's actually a very simple concept: *Be here now*. Be present in your life, as it is, without judgment.

DILIP'S hospital offered a course in mindfulness for its employees. Dilip thought it might help him be more present with his patients and family members. At first it was really hard for him to be able to sit quietly and observe his breath, or an object in the room, or the sensations in his body. His brain quickly began to judge and criticize his efforts and experience as "a waste of his time," or say that he "wasn't doing it right," or should be doing something more important. Dilip hadn't realized how noisy his inner world was, so full of self-criticism and judgment. He also became aware of how much his time was spent ruminating about things that were in the past or might happen in the future. He began to enjoy the calm and relief he sometimes experienced when he focused on the present moment, in the class and his life. Dilip found that he was interacting more with colleagues and patients at work, and was more attentive to his family at home. Being present and engaged in his life left less time for him to worry and ruminate fruitlessly and more time to engage with the things that really mattered to him. That didn't mean that he could always stay present in the moment; he still drifted into ruminating about work in the evenings, especially when he was very tired from work. Nonetheless, he continued to meditate and practice the mindfulness skills he had learned in the class.

Short Meditation: Mindful Breathing Script

Try this exercise throughout the day, when you find a few minutes to reconnect to yourself and the present moment. You can find many variations of this exercise online or in the meditation apps recommended in the resources section of this book. You can do this anywhere—at your desk at work, on the subway during your commute, waiting in line at the grocery store. Just take a few minutes to reconnect with the breath and the present moment. Noticing the breath allows us to shift our attention to the present moment, to what is happening right now, in our most essential experience of life—breathing.

Meditation is not something that we aim to do perfectly. The goal is simply to remain open and curious to our experiences. One common misconception about meditation is that we are supposed to stop thinking.

While it is true that it is possible to find moments of stillness when the mind quiets its constant chatter, it's important to remember that the job of the mind is to think, and it is most likely that that's what it's going to keep doing while we meditate. The point is to be a witness to our mind without judgment and with compassion. Meditation is a practice, and the benefits increase the more we do it. Some days we may find relaxation, some days we may be bombarded with thoughts. The goal is to simply be present with whatever thoughts or feelings arise with acceptance and curiosity.

Start by sitting in a comfortable position. Allow your eyes to close or remain slightly open in a gentle gaze. It can sometimes be helpful to smile gently to remind yourself that this exercise can be lighthearted, playful, and kind.

Sit upright with intention, aware of where your legs touch the chair, how the air feels on your skin, noticing the sounds in the room.

Notice as you sit here that you are breathing. Bring your attention to the gentle motion in your nose and throat and chest that happens without thinking, without effort. Notice how it feels as the air passes into your nose and fills your lungs, and then flows out again at its own pace. Don't try to change the speed of your breathing as you breathe in and out. Just let it happen.

Notice how your chest expands as you breathe in, and how it contracts as you breathe out. Sit quietly noticing these things, how the air feels cooler going in and warmer as you breathe out.

It is okay to notice other sensations—a pain in your neck, a tickle in your throat, the sounds outside, or the smells coming from the kitchen. Notice them without judgment, and then return your attention to the breath. If your mind wanders to a thought, plan, or worry, you don't need to push it away. Just gently let it go, and return again to the breath.

If it is helpful to you, you can count each breath—breathing in and breathing out, count one; breathing in and out, count two—until you reach ten, and then begin again at one.

Continue breathing and noticing what comes up for five minutes or so, returning always to the breath. When you are ready, gently open your eyes, stretch your legs, perhaps thank yourself for giving yourself this gift of mindful presence, and return to your day.

Mindfulness in Everyday Life

Mindfulness exercises help us practice present-moment awareness in different ways and settings. Mindfulness doesn't need to be practiced while sitting still in a pristine meditation room or awe-inspiring natural setting. In fact, practicing mindfulness in our real lives and mundane moments allows us to learn that we can tolerate whatever life delivers, enabling us to be grounded in ourselves and our lives in the present moment.

Here are some simple mindfulness exercises you can practice anytime and anywhere throughout your day.

Exercise 1:
Get Grounded in the Present Moment

Pause in this moment and notice:
One thing that you can see.
One thing that you can hear.
One thing that you can smell.
One thing that you can feel.

Exercise 2:
This Is What I Am Experiencing Right Now

Simply stop at any moment in your day and notice where you are and what you are experiencing by saying, "This is what I am experiencing right now." Breathe in. Breathe out. You've done it! You have made time for mindfulness in the middle of your busy day! And just doing this a few times a day can have a big impact on how you experience yourself and your life. Try it for a few days and see if you notice anything different.

Exercise 3:
Daily Mindful Activity

Choose one activity that you do every day and commit to doing it mindfully. The activity can be anything—brushing your teeth, washing the dishes, eating breakfast, vacuuming the kitchen floor, showering, sitting on the bus on your way to work. Choose one activity and commit to trying to engage in it mindfully for two minutes. Be curious about your experience as you notice all the little details you're usually too busy to notice. Notice how the toothpaste tastes on your tongue, or how the toast crumbs fall onto your plate when you pick up the toast. Maybe you will notice how the man with the newspaper smiles when you sit down next to him. You get the idea. Don't worry if you notice that your mind wanders to other things; that is just another thing to notice. Try to do this daily for a week, with curiosity and kindness.

Exercise 4:
Mindful Walking

The idea that we need to be sitting still to be mindful often keeps us from making time for mindfulness practices. Mindful walking is simply choosing to use the time you are walking to pay attention to the experience of walking. Often when we are walking or exercising, we listen to music or plug ourselves into a podcast or audiobook, either to make the task more interesting or to zone out. Mindful walking or exercising is a way to check in, rather than check out, when we are engaged in a movement task. Maybe you can choose to be mindful for the first two to five minutes of your walk. While you are walking, pay attention to how the ground feels beneath your feet, the sound of the traffic, the smell of the blooming flowers, or the feeling of the sunlight on your face. You might even silently name things as you notice them: "horn honking," "jasmine scent," "sunshine," and so on. Trying to do this for just a part of a walk or workout can change the experience from one that you feel like you need to check out of to one that allows you to check in and be present.

Exercise 5:
Cultivating Awareness
(An Alternative to Meditation)

I often hear that people "can't" or "don't like to" meditate. I will often suggest that they try doing this exercise instead. (This is a modified version of a practice described by Rachel Naomi Remen in her book *My Grandfather's Blessings.*) Before you go to bed, find a quiet place to reflect with a journal or piece of paper. Look back on the day and think about something that *surprised* you and write it down, reflecting on why it was surprising. Then look back on your day and consider one thing that *inspired* you. Write it down and describe why. And last, think of one thing that *touched* you. Write it down and describe why. This simple practice gives us a moment to reflect and appreciate what may have seemed like an ordinary or even awful day. Every time I do this practice, I am surprised by the moments I find that would have been lost without this small moment of reflection.

Manage Your Emotions

Mindfulness may help you feel better and more relaxed, but that is not the only goal of mindfulness. Practicing mindfulness in our real lives, in our less-than-perfect moments, is an even more important and impactful application of mindfulness skills. Mindfulness allows us to be present in our difficult moments with acceptance and self-compassion. One of the goals of practicing mindfulness is to be present in your life no matter what feelings you are experiencing.

As we discussed in chapter 5, when we relate to our distressing emotions as dangerous, our brains are wired to react with avoidance and aversion. Mindfulness helps us shift from reacting to responding. Being present in our emotional experience allows us to be aware of the emotion and to choose whether we want to act on the urge generated by the emotion or respond in a more conscious way.

Our emotional experiences are like the weather. We don't get to know what emotional experiences we will have as we move through life, but we know for certain that these experiences will change and pass, allowing other experiences to take their place, regardless of what we do. The process of accepting our limited control and allowing emotions to pass through allows us to make space for the experience that we are getting rather than spend all of our energy resisting experiences that we do not want. If you search for the term "mountain meditation" online, you will find dozens of guided meditations that use this metaphor to guide listeners through a visualization of the listener as the mountain experiencing the weather passing over its landscape while it stands solidly, whether the weather is stormy, gloomy, or fair.

DILIP injured his knee playing tennis with a colleague. He consulted with his orthopedist and did the exercises prescribed by a physical therapist, but his knee continued to hurt when he moved. He found it hard to stay on his feet for long hours at work, and came home tired and irritable. He blamed himself for the injury and berated himself for the "carelessness" and "stupidity" that he believed caused it. His doctor had recommended physical therapy for the pain, but Dilip was unwilling to miss more work to make it to the appointments. His wife mentioned that he was more reactive and negative at home, reinforcing his sense that he was a terrible husband and father. He spent a lot of his time thinking about how things would have been if he hadn't injured his knee, and how he was always falling short.

4-7-8 Breathing Technique

The 4-7-8 breathing technique was popularized by Dr. Andrew Weil and is based on an ancient yoga practice called pranayama. I find this to be one of the simplest ways to teach people to use breathing techniques in their daily lives to help calm and regulate their emotions. Initially, you may want to practice this technique in a quiet place, sitting comfortably or standing.

Begin by taking a deep breath in through your nose, and then breathe out through your mouth with an audible *whoosh*. Now breathe through your nose to a count of four, then hold your breath for a count of seven, followed by a whooshing-out breath through your mouth to the count of eight.

Try that again: Breathe in through your nose to a count of four, then hold your breath for a count of seven, followed by a whooshing-out breath through your mouth to the count of eight. Try this a few times so you get the hang of it. You will find your own rhythm after a few tries. If you find that it is hard to hold your breath for seven, speed up your counting so that you are able to keep the breathing ratio of 4-7-8. Do this practice as many times as you like, for just a minute or for a more prolonged period.

This practice can be done anytime, anywhere. Some people find it helpful in moments of stress or anxiety as a way to calm their system, while others find it helpful at bedtime or when they wake up in the night. It is something that is always available to us whenever we need to center and ground ourselves with our breath. Perhaps when you are sitting at your desk or in the car on the way to work. The technique of 4-7-8 breathing is something that you can practice and make a part of your mindfulness tool kit to help manage your emotions.

Body Scan

This next strategy is a short meditation that can help you relax and reconnect with your body. You can read the script a few times and narrate for yourself, or listen to a similar guided meditation from one of the apps and websites listed in the resources section of this book. This body scan can be done any time, sitting or standing. Some people find it helpful before bed to wind down.

Begin by taking a few deep breaths. Notice how your breath feels going in and out through your nostrils.

Notice how it feels to be sitting or lying down, where your body touches the chair or cushion. Notice how your feet feel. Are they hot or cold, tense or relaxed?

Move your attention to your legs, noticing any sensations there, any weight or pressure as they rest. From there, move your attention to your hips and back. How do they feel? What do you notice?

Now move to your abdomen and stomach. What do you feel in this area? Is your stomach full or empty? Does your abdomen move up and down with your breath?

Notice your arms and hands as you continue to breathe. If your hands are tense, let them soften and relax.

Next, notice your chest as it rises and falls with your breath. Is there any tightness or sensation there? Can you allow the tightness to soften as you breathe? Now move to your shoulders. What do you notice there?

Now move your attention to your neck. Can you allow any tenseness or tightness to leave your body through your breath? Notice your jaw. Is it tense or tight? Can you allow that tension to relax as you move your attention to your head, and then back to your breath?

Rest quietly, noticing what it is like to be in your whole body. Continue to breathe, noticing your breath and resting in your body quietly for as long as you wish.

Once you have done this short body scan a few times, you will know it well enough to do it without guidance, perhaps lengthening it and making it your own. Some people find that certain areas of their body are particularly tense and may want to spend more time checking in with that area in greater detail.

Key Takeaways

- Mindfulness practices teach us how to be here, in the present moment, without judgment, and with kindness.

- Mindfulness practice asks us to sit with our experience as it unfolds, whether the moment is difficult or pleasurable or tedious.

- These skills allow us to build our repertoire of ways to relate to our emotional world flexibly and compassionately.

- Mindfulness is an important part of current CBT treatment protocols such as MBCT (mindfulness-based cognitive therapy).

- Mindfulness may help you feel better and more relaxed, but that is not the only goal of mindfulness.

- Practicing mindfulness in our real lives, in our less-than-perfect moments, allows us to be present no matter what feelings we are experiencing.

- Mindfulness doesn't change our emotions; it changes the way we relate to our emotions.

Part Four

Change Your Behaviors

================================

Goals help us orient ourselves toward the things that matter to us and are essential tools for changing the behavior that feeds our depression. This next chapter will start with small goals that you can commit to as a way to begin your goal-setting practice. As you get a clearer picture of what matters to you and what changes you would like to make in your life, you will begin to identify the larger goals that you would like to work on day by day, and consider the pros and cons of taking the steps necessary to meet them. Then, in chapter 8, we will unpack the tasks and actions that need to happen to meet these goals and create action plans. Goals and action plans are a critical part of CBT for depression. Setting goals and making an action plan for achieving them allows you to move toward change in your life in simple, achievable steps.

chapter 7

be goal oriented

Depression is sustained and perpetuated by behaviors such as experiential avoidance, social withdrawal, and procrastination. That is why CBT for depression emphasizes goal setting, to help you mobilize and begin to choose actions and activities that will lead you back toward the things that bring meaning and purpose to your life. This chapter will teach you ways to use goal setting to challenge the behaviors that feed your depression.

FOR **ANTOINE**, depression was a familiar experience. He had struggled with feelings of worthlessness and hopelessness since high school. He had found a medication that helped a little, and did some therapy to talk about his life, but every setback would leave him feeling defeated and discouraged. He began to assume that was "just the way he was." The most recent setback had coincided with him getting a promotion at his job as an aide in a preschool classroom. He had been asked to start an arts and crafts curriculum for the youngest children, aged two to three. Although this was an opportunity for Antoine to expand his experience, he felt overwhelmed by the challenge and couldn't get himself to begin devising a curriculum or plan. Antoine feared that he wasn't going to be able to meet the challenges of the new position. He started arriving to work later than usual and missing meetings with staff. He worried constantly about losing his job and disappointing his supervisor. He felt guilty that he had taken the position when he was clearly not up to the challenge. When he arrived at my office, he had missed several days of work and had barely been able to leave the house.

Setting Goals

As I mentioned earlier, depression is better described as something that you do, rather than something that you have. Goal setting is a way to support you as you begin to *do* your way through your depression. Each time you set and achieve a goal, you have new evidence to prove that you are able to move forward with your life and through this difficult time.

There are many strategies that can help you stay motivated and make your goals more manageable. Simply having a goal and setting your intention to move toward it can increase your motivation and confidence that you can achieve the goal. Remember to use the self-compassion skills we practiced earlier to encourage yourself and remind yourself that the aim is progress, not perfection. Research shows that simply taking a small step toward a goal increases your commitment and motivation to keep moving forward. Often people think goals need to be big, ambitious undertakings that will require a major overhaul of their lives. These kinds of unrealistic expectations can set people up for disappointment and discouragement and overlook the important fact that every accomplishment is the result of many smaller steps.

Initially we will focus on these smaller steps that can lead to larger outcomes. Rather than committing to going to the gym five days per week when you haven't been to the gym in years, maybe you can focus on a step toward that goal, like going to the gym to sign up for a membership or dusting off that elliptical machine in the guest room and doing a 10-minute workout. These smaller goals are more likely to culminate in the long-term changes you are hoping to make in your life. It is easy to overlook that taking a 10-minute walk today is a significant increase if you haven't been exercising at all!

When we set a goal and accomplish it, we build evidence to combat our negative automatic thinking and internal beliefs. It can be hard to get started, but once you begin to orient yourself toward a few tangible goals that emphasize the areas of your life that are contributing to your depression, you will begin to see that you, not your depression, are in the driver's seat. If you recognize that depression has led you to become more socially isolated, you may make a goal of reaching out to friends and family members more often, or joining a meditation group or club. If you now recognize that oversleeping is making you late for work, you might make a goal of setting an extra alarm or asking for a family member help you get up on time.

Let's start with a daily goal that you would be willing to commit to right now. It could be as simple as making your bed every morning, or sending one text to a friend, or writing three things you are grateful for in your journal. Once you have chosen your daily practice, make sure that you keep track of whether or not you have met the goal each day. It may help to record it in your phone or in a journal. This practice of committing to a small daily goal will begin your goal-setting practice. Don't get discouraged if you miss a day. Setbacks are normal and offer more practice to make the choice to return to your goal. Just begin again the next day with the intention of achieving the goal you have set for yourself.

Once you have practiced setting and achieving these small goals, you can move on to creating life goals that are inspired by what is most important to you. Motivation is directly linked to how much we care about the goal we are moving toward. When we reflect on the things that give our lives meaning and purpose, we can begin to narrow down what we want more or less of in our lives. For instance, Antoine cared deeply about his work and making a difference in the lives of the children in his class. One of his goals was to make it to work every day so that he could show up for and meet the needs of his students.

If you're struggling with depression, you know that mobilizing and motivation are challenging. Everyone struggles to get going on a new task or goal sometimes, but when we are depressed, it can be especially challenging. If you have a clear understanding of why your goals are important to you, you will be able to orient toward these goals not because you "should," but because they matter to you. When you are depressed, you may feel like the depression is your fault, and that if you would just do all the things people are saying you "should" do, you wouldn't be struggling so much. This unhelpful thinking feeds the depression and makes it even harder to get started. Try to switch your "should" statements to "could" statements that allow you to recognize that making changes is a choice, one that you are making to move forward in your life. Think of something you have been telling yourself you should do—maybe exercising more or returning that email from an old friend. Try saying "I could" do it rather than "I should." This seems small, but words can be a very powerful way to reframe the way we are approaching a task. This little trick shifts the task from a guilt-ridden burden to a choice that you are making because it is something that matters to you.

ANTOINE went to summer camp every summer when he was younger. He loved camp, especially swimming in the lake. When he got older, he was allowed to swim across the lake with his friends to a beach on the other side. There was a bright red raft floating in the water near the beach, which was clearly visible from the other side of the lake. Antoine would find that as he swam toward the beach with his face in the water, he would move slightly off course. He learned to stop periodically to check his progress and reorient back toward the red raft. No matter how far he might veer off course, he could always reorient to the dock by stopping to assess his progress.

What's Important to You?

Our values work in the same way that the red raft helped Antoine orient toward the shore he was trying to get to. Your core values help you determine what you want to do in life and orient you toward your goals, even when you inevitably drift off course (Hayes, et al. 2006). If you love your work, maybe achievement or leadership is a value for you. If you love being a parent, maybe caregiving or nurturing is a core value for you. If you love running marathons, maybe endurance or self-improvement is a core value for you.

Look at the table on page 105 and take some time to reflect on how you might rank the four life domains in importance to you. Read the list of qualities for each domain and notice which ones seem particularly relevant and important to you. Other qualities may come up, too. It might be useful to write these qualities down for yourself so you can return to them when you face obstacles or feel like you're veering off course.

Life Domains Table

RELATIONSHIPS, FAMILY, AND FRIENDS	☐ Caregiving ☐ Community ☐ Leadership ☐ Nurturing ☐ Connection ☐ Honesty	☐ Dependability ☐ Loyalty ☐ Helpfulness ☐ Service to others ☐ Other:
HEALTH, WELL-BEING, AND SELF-DEVELOPMENT	☐ Balance ☐ Harmony ☐ Well-being ☐ Strength	☐ Endurance ☐ Self-improvement ☐ Self-reliance ☐ Other:
WORK, HOME, AND SCHOOL	☐ Excellence ☐ Teamwork ☐ Service ☐ Leadership ☐ Knowledge	☐ Curiosity ☐ Mastery ☐ Achievement ☐ Other:
CREATIVITY AND PLAY	☐ Beauty ☐ Imagination ☐ Innovation ☐ Openness ☐ Independence	☐ Freedom ☐ Fun ☐ Curiosity ☐ Other:

Now that you have identified the domains of your life that are most important to you and the qualities that you want to bring to these domains, let's try to create goals that are aligned with these things. If you identified dependability with your family and friends as a quality that you value, how does depression affect your relationships? Does depression lead you to isolate yourself and not be there for your loved ones in the way you value? If imagination and curiosity are qualities that you value, how does depression keep you from expressing these in your life?

Can you think of some actions that might move you toward these domains and qualities that you value? For instance, Antoine ranked the Work, Home, and School domain as most important, and the qualities he valued as a part of this domain were curiosity and mastery. A goal that he devised to move toward these qualities was to research art projects that he could do with his new classroom.

What are some concrete goals that might move you toward the qualities you value in the domain you ranked number one?

Why It Works: Reflecting on your values and what's important to you can help motivate you to work toward your goals, which is a powerful tool in changing the behavior that contributes to depression.

ANTOINE realized that one of the goals that he would like to commit to was to research and apply for graduate programs in early childhood development. Every time he would consider this goal, he would feel overwhelmed by the many tasks that might be involved in achieving this goal, and would convince himself that he just wasn't "grad school material." Then we began to use the SMART acronym to define a goal that he could work toward without getting overwhelmed. For the next week, Antoine committed to a SMART goal: calling a friend from college who was at a psychology graduate program and asking her about the program she was in. The following week, Antoine was able to come up with another specific goal: to email his college adviser about his interest in graduate school and ask her for advice on how he should approach the process. As Antoine built his confidence in his ability to move toward SMART goals, we began to create a more complex plan that outlined the steps he would need to take to meet his goal of applying to some graduate programs by the following spring.

Creating SMART Goals

SMART is a commonly used acronym, sometimes attributed to George T. Doran, for creating goals that are well-defined and measurable. This acronym is a helpful way to make sure that the goals are:

Specific

Measurable

Action-oriented

Relevant and

Time-bound.

Use this as you define the goals that you want to work on as a way to move your way through your depression and into a life filled with more meaning and purpose.

Reflect on the goals you came up with in the last strategy exercise. Choose one and we will use the SMART goal acronym to further define the goal.

Specific: Is this goal specific and tangible? Are there clear steps that you can take to achieve this goal?

Measurable: Can you track your progress on this goal in a tangible way?

Action-oriented: Is this goal something that is in your power to move toward and reach by taking deliberate action? Is this goal attainable with effort and planning?

Relevant: Is this goal aligned to the values you identified as important to you in this chapter? Is this goal relevant to the things in your life that matter to you?

Time-bound: Is this goal time-limited and measurable? Can you schedule and track the tasks that need to happen to achieve this goal?

Now reconsider your goal. Does it meet all of the SMART criteria? If not, how can you change the goal to make it a SMART goal? Fine-tune your goal using the SMART acronym.

Why It Works: Creating SMART goals is a way to focus your energy and efforts on goals that will have the most impact in helping you move through your depression and fill your life with more meaning and purpose.

Get Unstuck

Setting goals seems simple, but often the path toward our goals can be littered with obstacles and struggles that we can't foresee. It can be helpful to anticipate that there will be pitfalls, so that we don't get discouraged when they inevitably happen. You have created goals that are SMART and will move you toward the things that matter to you, so you are off to a good start. Nonetheless, obstacles will happen, and we can consider some common reasons that we end up feeling stuck or thrown off course.

Common reasons we get stuck or thrown off course are:

Not feeling "ready" to change: Sometimes we assume that we can't begin until we feel totally "ready." If that were the case, we would never begin! If you are falling into this kind of emotional reasoning, try to remember that you are *doing* your way forward, not *feeling* your way forward. Feelings of resistance are a normal and natural response to anything new, but you are still in the driver's seat, and you can choose to move beyond your resistance and toward your life. Do something even when you don't have the feeling that you are ready. Often it is taking action to change our behavior that is the first step in changing how we feel. Courage is not the absence of fear, it is choosing to take action even when we are afraid.

Viewing setbacks as failures: Setbacks are always going to happen, even when you have made a detailed plan. When you mistake setbacks for failures, you give yourself permission to give up, and then beat yourself up for failing. Expecting setbacks and having some self-compassion for yourself when they happen can help you move on rather than give up.

Underestimating how hard it will be: Research shows that people often underestimate how difficult a task will be and get discouraged when the task is harder than they expected. Try to be realistic about how difficult the task might be, and prepare to adjust your expectations.

Giving up too early because you aren't seeing results: It is important that your SMART goal is measurable, but allow enough time to begin to see results. Don't quit, and use your problem-solving skills to consider what might be going on. Were your expectations realistic? Do you need more time before you will see results?

Sabotaging yourself when you are reaching the finish line: Initially we fear not reaching our goal, and when we realize we are close to it, we may have mixed feelings about that, too! Sometimes getting close to accomplishing our goal can heighten our fears of failing and losing what we are so close to having. Take time to name and express your feelings so they don't disrupt your progress.

This chapter outlined four domains of life (p. 105) that encompass many of the things in life that bring us meaning and well-being. Whether you value family and relationships, health and well-being, work and school, or creativity and play, you know the domains in your life that are most important to you. You also learned what qualities you most value within these domains. Use these to orient yourself when you are finding it difficult to mobilize and move toward your goals. Often what we need to do to move toward a more satisfying life requires us to do things that look difficult, tedious, or unappealing. When we remember that we are doing these things because they will move our lives toward what matters to us, we are able to stay on course.

ANTOINE felt discouraged when he realized that he had to take a few extra classes before he could apply to graduate school. He first thought about giving up, telling himself "It's too hard," and "I can't do it," and "Maybe it's just not meant to be." But then he tried to remember that his goal was to move toward a career that had meaning and purpose, and that required him to do the things necessary to make that possible. He reminded himself that he'd taken plenty of classes before and he knew it was something he could do, even if it was challenging. Using the tools outlined in this chapter, Antoine was able to examine the obstacles he was facing and work toward what really mattered to him.

Overcome Goal Obstacles

When you are feeling stuck, this is a strategy you can use to realign with your values and find the motivation to keep going. Think about one of your goals and reflect on the following questions:

- Why is this goal important?
- What are the benefits of achieving this goal?
- Are there any potential costs of achieving this goal?

- What obstacles might get (or are currently getting) in your way? List any obstacles you can think of, along with solutions that may help you overcome these obstacles.

OBSTACLES	SOLUTIONS
I want to work on writing my novel, but I'm too tired after work.	Go to bed by 10 p.m. so I can wake up one hour earlier to write in the morning when I have the most energy.
I can't motivate myself to exercise.	Ask my neighbor if she wants to go for a walk with me twice a week so the plan will hold me accountable.
I'm feeling isolated and lonely, but I can't bring myself to reach out.	Text my two closest friends and ask them to check in on me every day this week.

Is there a different way you could approach your goal that might make it easier to accomplish? For instance, doing it at a different time of day or doing it in smaller increments. (Sometimes just changing things up offers a new perspective that can help us get over the hump.)

Are there people you can ask for support or help achieving this goal?

Why It Works: When we reorient ourselves toward our goals and the values behind them, we can find motivation to keep working toward them, even if we have gotten off track. When we are able to look at our obstacles realistically, we often find that there are solutions we had not thought of.

Key Takeaways

- CBT for depression emphasizes goal setting to help you mobilize and begin to choose actions and activities that will lead you toward meaning and well-being.

- Setting goals and making a plan for achieving them allows you to move toward change in your life in simple, achievable steps.

- If we choose goals that are oriented toward things that matter to us, we are more likely to be able to make the changes necessary to move forward.

- SMART goals are Specific, Measurable, Action-oriented, Relevant, and Time-bound.

- It is natural to get stuck and lose motivation sometimes, but CBT teaches us tools to get back on track and overcome our obstacles.

chapter 8

act now

This chapter will focus on ways for you to mobilize and begin to do the things that you know will help you feel better and more engaged with your life. This will not be easy, but it is the most effective way to improve your mood and move you back into a fuller life. Often, this will require you to engage in "opposite action," a term that describes the concept of doing the opposite of what the depression is telling you to do (Linehan 1993). For instance, if your depressed mood tells you to isolate from friends and family, or to stay in bed rather than go to work, we are going to encourage you to try to do the opposite of that. This chapter will help you learn strategies to help you begin to commit to and plan for actions that will move you through your depression and back into your life.

KAITLYN was struggling to get out of bed in the morning. There just didn't seem to be anything worth getting up for. She was failing her physics class, was a week behind handing in her senior thesis proposal, and was too embarrassed to reach out to her friends because she was such a mess. She used to enjoy waking up early to go to the early yoga class in the fitness center or to go for a run, but by began staying in her room watching Netflix or ruminating about all of the schoolwork she hadn't gotten done.

She wasn't replying to texts from her friends and family because she knew that they would ask her how she was, or try to get her to face all of the things she was avoiding. When she finally turned up in my office as a referral from her academic advisor, Kaitlyn had little hope that she would ever feel "normal" again. She appeared in my office in what looked like pajama pants and a sweatshirt. She curled up into a ball on my couch and yawned audibly before putting her head back down on her knees. She answered my questions in a quiet voice, admitting with some embarrassment that this was the first time she had left her room in a week. She said that she was sure she would have slept through our meeting if the RA in the dorm had not woken her up and walked her to my office. When I asked her how the RA knew to do this, she admitted that she had asked her to the day before, when the RA had stopped in to check on her. When I congratulated her on getting the support she needed to take care of herself, she didn't realize that she was utilizing what many deem to be one of the most effective interventions in CBT, called "behavioral activation."

Activate Your Life

The CBT model considers how our thoughts, emotions, and behaviors feed and perpetuate depression. While many emphasize the cognitive aspects of depression (distorted thinking, negative internal beliefs, thinking errors, and so on), research has found that behavioral activation may be the active ingredient that makes CBT so effective for treating depression (Jacobson et al. 1996). Similar to the vicious cycle of negative thinking we reviewed in chapter 4, what we do, or in some cases what we don't do, can generate a cycle that makes our depression worse. Kaitlyn's depression left her feeling exhausted, leading her to withdraw from her social circle and stay in bed, which made her feel even more hopeless and disengaged from her life.

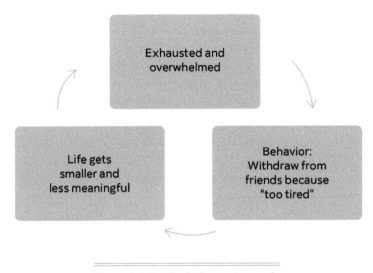

Figure 8.1 Kaitlyn's depression cycle

Behavioral activation aims to reverse this vicious cycle to lead us back into a more meaningful and purposeful life. That can be as simple as using the concept of "opposite action," doing the opposite of what our depression is telling us to do. For instance, when Kaitlyn felt tired and thought she wouldn't have the energy to see her friends, she tried to do the opposite instead, leading her to expand her world and feel a little bit better.

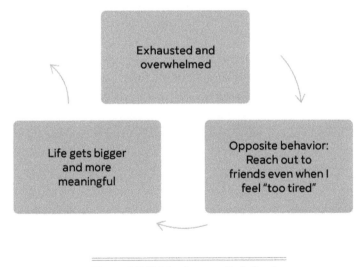

Figure 8.2 Kaitlyn's opposite behavior

One of the skills that we will practice is behavior monitoring, to become more aware of how our behaviors impact how we feel. Then we will begin to consider our unique situation and what might be most helpful for us to motivate behavioral change. Some of us may be motivated by the life domains and principles we isolated in the last chapter. Others may recognize that having social support from and accountability to family and friends is helpful as they begin to act their way out of depression. Most of us will find activity scheduling and setting up rewards for making changes to our behavior to be helpful ways to begin reversing the vicious cycle of depression.

Even the smallest changes can have a cascading effect on our lives. What are you willing to do to begin your behavioral activation plan? Would it be making one phone call to a friend, taking a shower first thing in the morning, making your bed (found to be correlated with improved mood), or taking a walk around the block? Choose one thing and make a commitment to yourself that you will try to achieve it in the next 24 hours. Ask people in your life to support you in doing this goal and give them permission to help you do so. Starting small and getting social support are your first steps toward behaving your way to a better mood.

KAITLYN was a little overwhelmed by the prospect of changing the way she was doing things. The choices that she was making made sense to her. One of the first things I asked her to do was to start tracking what she was doing during the day and rate her mood for each activity in an activity-tracking diary. If any of the activities in her diary were accompanied by feelings of accomplishment or pleasure, she would put an A or P next to them. After a few weeks, Kaitlyn was able to use this diary to investigate what activities improved or worsened her mood. We paid special attention to the activities marked with A and P, noticing that Kaitlyn's mood was much better when she was with her friends in the common room of the dorm watching movies (marked with a P) and when she handed in a homework assignment on time for her physics class (marked with an A). We used these items as clues for what kinds of activities might help improve her mood, and created a list of possible pleasurable activities Kaitlyn could do. Then we made a plan to schedule these activities intentionally into her days the same way she might schedule other routine activities like classes and meals. This helped her make a practice of scheduling pleasurable activities into each of her days.

Game Plan

One of the simplest and most powerful behavioral activation techniques is scheduling fun and rewarding activities into your daily life. By doing this, we ensure that the activities we *have* to do are balanced with pleasurable activities we *want* to do. Use the list and exercises given here to generate your own list of activities you would find pleasurable, and then schedule them into your life. Think of these as important appointments you are making with yourself.

Possible Pleasurable Activities List:

- Read a book
- Work in the garden
- Watch a movie
- Play a video game
- Spend time with friends
- Spend time with family
- Cook a nice meal
- Take a walk
- Exercise
- Take a warm bath
- Listen to a podcast
- Help someone
- Call an old friend
- Clean out a drawer or closet
- Bake something
- Engage in a hobby or interest
- Listen to music
- Play a board game
- Write, paint, sew
- Take a hike
- Sing, dance, play
- Journal
- Write a letter
- Entertain friends
- Get or give a massage
- Take a hike
- Play with a pet
- Practice gratitude
- Meditate
- Other:

Exercise 1:
Daily Activity Diary

For each hour that you are awake, log what you are doing and rate your depressed mood from 0 to 100 (0 means no depressed mood and 100 is the most depressed mood that you have ever experienced) in your journal or planner. Place an A next to activities that elicit feelings of accomplishment and a P next to activities that are accompanied by feelings of pleasure.

What are you doing when your mood is rated as particularly bad compared to other times of the day?

What are the activities that you notice are accompanied by improved mood ratings and/or marked with an A or P? How can you schedule more activities like these into your daily life?

Exercise 2:

Think about activities that are pleasurable now or have been in the past. Rate how easy it would be to integrate each of these activities into your life, and consider potential obstacles.

ACTIVITY	HOW DIFFICULT TO INTEGRATE INTO DAILY LIFE (1 IS NOT AT ALL DIFFICULT AND 10 IS VERY DIFFICULT)	POTENTIAL OBSTACLES TO INTEGRATING THIS ACTIVITY IN YOUR LIFE
Example: Walk the dog	7	I will be too tired, I won't want to see the neighbors without showering
Other Activities:		

Now schedule one or two pleasurable activities into each day for the next week. Consider the level of difficulty you rated each activity and try to choose activities that are rated less difficult to get you started. Move to more difficult items as you get the hang of this. Review the obstacles you list for each item and make a plan to minimize these obstacles.

Why It Works: Taking action to schedule pleasurable activities into our daily lives improves our mood and helps us show up for the things that are important to us.

INITIALLY, **KAITLYN** couldn't understand why I was encouraging her to do things that seemed difficult and uncomfortable. After a few weeks of tracking her activities and mood, Kaitlyn noticed that her mood was particularly low when she stayed in bed in the morning and skipped class, and when she followed what her former boyfriend was doing on social media. We decided that these were good things to consider how to improve or eliminate. Kaitlyn agreed to try to get up at the same time every morning to allow time to shower before class, to delete Twitter and Instagram from her phone, and to talk to her friends about how they could encourage her to go out more. She continued to track her activities and mood in her activity diary, and monitored how these changes improved her mood ratings. She learned from her setbacks (it was really hard to stay off social media!) and was motivated to continue making changes to her life.

Reduce or Eliminate Activities That Make You Feel Worse

Use your activity diary to determine some of the times and activities when your mood is particularly low.

1. What are these activities and are there ways that you can reduce or eliminate these activities from your day?

   Kaitlyn: Stalking ex-boyfriend on social media (mood rating: 50)
   Woke up late and missed class (40)
   Staying at home instead of going out with my friends (40)

2. What do you need to do to reduce or eliminate these activities from the coming week? Are there ways to schedule alternative activities or get some support from friends to change these things?

   Kaitlyn: Delete social media accounts or change passwords so they are harder to access
   Ask my RA to knock on my door to make sure I am awake before class
   Ask my friends to come and get me even when I say I don't want to go out

3. What are the things you need to do to make sure that you reduce or eliminate these things from your week?

   Kaitlyn: Actually delete social media apps from phone
   Talk to my RA about waking me up
   Tell my friends about what I am learning in therapy and ways they can help me go out with them more often

Why It Works: Eliminating the activities and behaviors that make us feel bad is one of the simplest and most effective changes we can make to positively impact our mood.

WHEN I was a teenager, my mother took a class based on self-help guru Dale Carnegie's book *How to Make Friends and Influence People*. Whenever I would complain about being overwhelmed by school or work, she would respond with "Remember, you can only eat an elephant one bite at a time." I found the saying totally baffling, but now I realize Dale and my mom were on to something. This absurd idiom captures the concept that the only way to begin to tackle seemingly insurmountable tasks is by taking the first small bite, then the next, then the next—one bite at a time. When I used this term in a session, my patient giggled and said that she was a vegetarian. We changed the phrase to "You can only eat a watermelon one bite at a time," and used the phrase playfully throughout our work together.

Break It Down

The most effective way to approach daunting tasks is to chunk them into smaller, "bite-size" pieces. Once we have done this, we can tackle the tasks one at a time and move progressively toward our goal. As we accomplish each small step in the process, we collect more positive and encouraging "evidence" to combat our depression, and we gain motivation to keep going.

Pick one of your SMART goals (use a goal from the previous chapter or a new one). Now break it down into smaller pieces and consider the many steps that you will need to take to reach this goal, assigning a due date/time to each step. Writing tasks down can often relieve some of the pressure of holding everything in our heads, and the physical act of marking each completed step as done can act as extra encouragement.

Example:

Kaitlyn's SMART Goal: *Write term paper for sociology and hand it in at least one day early!*

Kaitlyn's Task List:

Task 1: *Choose topic and email to my professor for approval.*

Completion Date: *January 24th*

Task 2: *Find four sources of information on the topic at the library or online.*

Completion Date: *February 7th*

Task 3: *Read the articles and write notes*

Completion Date: *February 25th*

Task 4: *Write an outline of the paper and email to my professor for comments.*

Completion Date: *March 10th*

Task 5: *Begin to write the paper. Commit to spend at least four hours every weekend writing the paper.*

Completion Date: *April 10th*

Task 6: *Finish first draft and ask the teaching assistant if they will take a look and give me comments.*

Completion Date: *April 20th*

Task 7: *Edit paper and hand in before due date of May 5th.*

Completion Date: *May 4th*

Why It Works: Breaking a goal down into smaller, "bite-size" tasks helps us focus on what is more easily achievable, and keeps us from becoming overwhelmed and giving up.

Beat Procrastination

Procrastination is something that all of us do some of the time. It is a habitual response to performing tasks and responsibilities that we perceive to be adverse or difficult. We often assume that procrastination is a character flaw due to our lack of discipline and self-control. Not surprisingly, these negative assumptions tend to make us feel worse, leading to more negative thoughts and feelings.

Research on procrastination has found that procrastination is not the result of poor self-control, but is an attempt to manage negative emotions. The same fear system that perceives social threats as dangerous rather than simply uncomfortable also perceives the discomfort caused by mild to moderately adverse tasks to be dangerous. Procrastination is an avoidance response that provides short-term relief from the distress of unpleasant tasks and culminates in increased distress in the long term. Procrastination is an ineffective coping strategy to manage negative feelings about these tasks.

Many of the skills that we have already learned in this book are helpful for managing procrastination. Noticing our thinking when we are procrastinating is helpful because we will often discover the "permission thought" we are using to justify why we are procrastinating. Typical permission thoughts are:

"I'm going to do that later."

"I'm too tired to do that today."

"I need to do more research before I can get started."

"It's not going to take very long, so I can just do it at the last minute."

"I'm just not feeling it right now."

These thoughts support our procrastination plans and keep us from considering the costs of avoiding the tasks. When you notice these avoidance thoughts, use your thought-challenging skills and weigh the evidence before acting on them.

Remember the emotional regulation strategies we learned about in chapter 5? They are also useful for managing procrastination. We can remember them with the acronym TANS, which stands for Thought restructuring, Acceptance, Normalizing, and Self-compassion. Let's consider how these four coping strategies can be applied to procrastination.

Thought restructuring: Thought restructuring enables us to consider alternative ways to think about the tasks we are avoiding. If we are able to step back from a situation and consider how accurate and helpful our thinking is, we are likely to change how we feel about a situation.

Acceptance: Acceptance asks us to make space for the emotional distress that the tasks we are facing are causing us. It is the opposite of avoidance. Rather than reacting to distressing tasks by pushing them out of our minds or ignoring them, we allow the feelings to be present and inform how we choose to proceed. One way to do this is to be curious about the emotions you are experiencing. Does the task make you feel fearful and anxious or bored and resentful? The emotions we experience when we are facing difficult or even mundane tasks provide us with critical information about what the task means to us. Acceptance also helps us learn that if we allow distress to be present as it is, it is likely to change and pass through like stormy weather, after which we can return to the tasks we need to face.

Normalizing: Normalizing is particularly helpful with the distress that procrastination causes us. *All* of us procrastinate some of the time. It is a part of the human experience if we are living, working, and pursuing our goals. Acknowledging this when we are procrastinating challenges the idea that procrastinating is a weakness or character flaw.

Self-compassion: Self-compassion allows us to shift from being self-critical to having compassion for ourselves in a moment of distress and suffering. In a recent study, researchers found that students who forgave themselves for procrastinating on an exam were less likely to procrastinate for the next exam (Wohl, Pychyl, and Bennet, 2010). It seems that forgiving ourselves for procrastinating helps us move forward and beyond the setback. I find the concept of "progress, not perfection" to be very helpful when working on procrastination. We will never be able to resist the urge to procrastinate every time, but we can move past it rather than dwelling on a setback. Self-compassion allows us to view ourselves and our situations with the nonjudgmental eyes of a trusted friend.

Something that can also help motivate you to complete a task is to choose a reward to give yourself when it is done. What is something pleasurable that you could look forward to and would be an added incentive to reaching your goal? It doesn't have to be something big, and it should be something that is not harmful to you. (For instance, rewarding yourself with an alcoholic drink may not be the best choice if alcohol is something you use to avoid dealing with your depression.

Sweet treats might not be the best reward if eating healthier is one of your goals.) Some ideas of healthy rewards might be playing video games or watching a movie, going somewhere fun for the weekend, eating lunch outside instead of at your desk, giving yourself a home spa day, getting a massage, buying yourself some flowers, spending an hour away from your phone or computer, taking your dog for an extra-long walk, or anything from your pleasurable activities list. The options are endless!

KAITLYN knew that the deadline for the first draft of her senior thesis was a week away and that she had not finished two important sections. Every day she would commit to spending at least a few hours on her thesis, but she would always find other things that distracted her from her goal. As the deadline approached, she considered dropping the class and graduating late rather than facing the task. When we began working together, her deadline was just a week away, and she had not begun the work she needed to do to finish. We discussed how procrastination was an avoidance response, and how we needed a way to help her begin to approach the task. We also discussed social support that might be helpful to her as she tried to make the deadline. Kaitlyn agreed to chunk the remaining sections into small bites that she could approach each day. She also agreed that she could email her thesis adviser and let her know her progress on the thesis and that she was struggling to make the deadline.

Procrastination Strategies Checklist

Use the following checklist and corresponding questions when you are procrastinating and/or avoiding tasks and commitments in your life.

Thought restructuring: What are some of the thoughts that you are having about the tasks you are avoiding? How accurate or helpful are these thoughts? Are there alternative ways of looking at the situation that may be more accurate or helpful?

Acceptance: What would it be like to accept the experience and the emotions you are having about the task(s)? Can you try to make space for these uncomfortable emotions? What is it like to allow this experience to be as it is, and also changeable and fleeting with time?

Normalizing: Procrastination and avoidance are things that happen to everyone. They do not make you weak or a bad person. Is this experience something that could only have happened to you, or is this something that could/does happen to most people at some time?

Self-compassion: Are you criticizing or judging yourself for procrastinating? What would it be like to forgive yourself for the way you are feeling and behaving right now? What might you have said to a friend in a similar situation?

Which of the strategies was most helpful to you in this situation?

Why It Works: The TANS acronym is a powerful tool to help us take the charge out of the fears and roadblocks that keep us from accomplishing our goals.

Set the Stage for Productivity

Creating an environment that reduces distractions and temptations and increases your ability to focus can literally set the stage for success.

- Create a work space that has everything you need to complete the task within arm's reach so that you won't get distracted by having to get up to find them.
- Use your work space consistently so your brain begins to associate this space with focused attention and work.
- Eliminate or remove distractions that will interfere with you getting to your work, such as phones, technology, people, noise, a messy desktop, and so on.

- Let the people who you share your environment with know when you are in work mode, and ask them to respect your need for time and quiet to work. Ask them to support you if they notice that you are getting distracted by other things.

Why It Works: Having an organized space dedicated to completing your tasks can help eliminate distractions and keep you focused. The state of our external physical space can have a big impact on how we feel internally.

Key Takeaways

- What we do, or in some cases what we *don't* do, can generate a vicious cycle that can make our depression worse.

- Research has found that behavioral activation is one of the active ingredients that makes CBT so effective for treating depression.

- Scheduling pleasurable activities and setting up rewards for making changes to our behavior are helpful ways to begin reversing the vicious cycle of depression.

- One of the simplest and most powerful behavioral activation techniques is scheduling fun and rewarding activities into your daily life.

- Even the smallest changes can have a cascading effect on our lives.

- The best way to approach daunting tasks is to chunk them into smaller, "bite-size" pieces.

- Procrastination is something that all of us do some of the time.

- Research on procrastination has found that procrastination is not the result of poor self-control, but is an attempt to manage negative emotions.

- Thought restructuring, Acceptance, Normalizing, and Self-compassion (TANS) are important coping strategies for managing procrastination.

- Creating an environment that reduces distractions and temptations and increases your ability to focus can literally set the stage for success.

Part Five

Stay Engaged

═══════════════════════════════════

If you have worked through the activities in this book and have started to feel better and more engaged in your life, it is easy to overlook the hard work and learning you have done. You might dive right back into your life and assume that the depression is behind you. While you absolutely deserve to enjoy your life and to do the things that bring you purpose and meaning, it is also important to make your mental health and well-being a priority moving forward. Knowing what you know now, consider ways to bring self-care and self-compassion into your daily life.

chapter 9

treat yourself

This book has been focused on CBT strategies and concepts that are effective ways of managing your depression and moving forward with your life. Learning to include yourself in the many responsibilities and chores that our lives require from us is a skill that will help you maintain your gains and continue to cultivate a rich and meaningful life. Self-care is not the same thing as self-compassion, but they are related. Self-care is committing to checking in with yourself every day to see if you have the things that you need to maintain a balanced and healthy life. When work, family, school, and other responsibilities are vying for our attention, we sometimes forget that caring for our health and well-being are essential parts of meeting our own needs and other responsibilities.

GRETA was really beginning to feel better, and felt ready to dive back into her busy life. She had increased her shifts at work, hoping to make up for the time she had missed when she was really struggling with her depression. She was eager to get back to the work that she loved and to help out the colleagues who had supported her over the past few months. Her kids were getting ready for summer vacation, and her husband would be traveling more for work again. She decided not to sign her children up for summer camps that year because of the financial hit her family had taken when she was missing so much work. She was juggling home and work responsibilities fairly well for the first few weeks, and then noticed that it was getting hard to get up in the mornings again. She missed a few therapy appointments because she felt that she needed to use the time to catch up on errands and household chores. She was staying up later than usual to fold laundry and get organized for the next day. She finally showed up to my office feeling exhausted and overwhelmed, disappointed that she "couldn't keep it together." When we looked at her current schedule and responsibilities, it was clear that there was one thing missing: time for her to take care of herself. For Greta, that meant time to exercise a few times per week, therapy, time to read before bed, and morning meditation, which helped her ground herself before she began her days. All four of these things had fallen to the bottom of her priority list.

Practice Self-Care

Self-care is a term that is often equated with occasional acts of self-indulgence to "treat yourself." When I bring up the concept in therapy, people often assume that I am recommending that they schedule a massage or pedicure. While I think these things are lovely, I am talking about a different kind of self-care. Self-care is an essential survival skill, not an occasional indulgence. My goal is to help people integrate self-care as a daily practice of doing things that help them to maintain health and balance in their daily lives. Sometimes this means doing things that are "good for us" rather than doing things that "feel good." For instance, self-care might be turning off Netflix at 10 p.m. so that you can wake up feeling refreshed, or choosing to eat a healthy breakfast at home in lieu of the sugary pastry at work. Self-care allows us to do the things we need to do to feel healthy and rested, so that we have the energy to do the other things that matter to us.

When we are depressed, it can be hard just to get out of bed in the morning, so practicing self-care may seem like yet another difficult thing to do. But I assure you, opportunities to practice self-care are easy to find. I like to use the acronym EASE (Exercise, Assertiveness, Self-compassion, Eating) to make it easy to access the areas of opportunity for practicing self-care.

It is important to start small when we begin to cultivate the practice of self-care. If you are finding it hard to get going, maybe self-care is simply acknowledging how hard it is right now and refraining from judging yourself for that. Say a kind word to yourself and resist the urge to criticize. Calling a friend to ask for help getting going or simply allowing yourself the comfort of petting your cat is also good self-care. Self-care can happen anywhere, especially in small private moments.

Here are some examples of self-care in practice:

- Taking a 10-minute walk around the block in the middle of the workday

- Committing to a weekly yoga class

- Saying no to a request to do something that will keep you from your real priorities

- Meditating for 10 minutes most mornings before work

- Asking for a time-out when you get overwhelmed in a conversation with a loved one

- Choosing to say no to that second drink at a party

- Prioritizing sleep

- Making time for things that you enjoy

- Allowing yourself a 10-second "breathing break" during a stressful meeting

- Choosing to reduce the amount of time you spend on social media

- Scheduling time for play

One essential aspect of self-care that is often overlooked is sleep. Getting adequate sleep is a very powerful tool for managing your mood and overall health. Research has found that improving your sleep can improve everything from depression and anxiety to diabetes and heart disease. Prioritizing sleep is very good self-care.

These are some simple guidelines for getting good sleep:

- Reduce napping

- Limit caffeine intake in the afternoon

- Exercise during the day if possible

- Schedule a time *before* bedtime (instead of when you are in bed) to mull over your day

- Have a wind-down

- Only use your bed for sleep (and sex)

- Make sure the bedroom is dark

- Eliminate electronics from the bedroom

GRETA began to recognize how her depression symptoms would get worse when she forgot to do the things that she needed to care for her health and well-being. She signed up for a yoga class that she could attend after work and on weekends. She also budgeted for a babysitter on the weeks that her husband was traveling, in order to give her some extra help with the children. She asked me if we could reschedule her therapy appointment so that it allowed her to do therapy during her lunch hour at work rather than having to leave work early every week. She committed to getting into bed every night by 10 p.m. so she would have time to read before she fell asleep. Finding meditation time was trickier. She decided to be flexible about finding times when she could meditate. Sometimes that meant meditating in her car at lunchtime at work or waking up 20 minutes before the kids. All of these changes required Greta to put her needs first and to advocate for those needs. That was a new skill for her, but she noticed that her life felt more manageable and balanced as a result.

Get Moving

Exercise is often referred to as a "transdiagnostic treatment," because it is correlated with improvement of just about every physical and psychological condition. We know that increased movement improves heart disease, diabetes, immune functioning, anxiety, depression, and ADHD, to name just a few. And the research is clear that nearly any type of exercise in relatively small amounts can have a profound impact on our mental and physical health and sense of well-being. A recent study done at Harvard found that regular exercise can be as effective as antidepressant medication for treating moderate depression symptoms. Nonetheless, when we are depressed, it can be really hard to get moving! Many of the symptoms of depression, including low energy, fatigue, hopelessness, and so on, make the idea of starting an exercise routine seem very daunting. The research shows that very small increases in movement have a huge impact on our mood, so it's fine to begin really small. Could you try a short walk around the block, five minutes on the treadmill, or stretching before you get into bed? All of these things will get you moving in a way that is likely to improve your mood.

It is important to choose things that you like doing so that you will be motivated to do them as a part of your daily routine. Some people like to do just one type of exercise regularly, and others like to have a variety of activities to keep them interested. Some people like to exercise alone, while others are motivated by social support like committing to going to yoga with a friend or walking with a neighbor. I've provided a list of different options for getting moving. Find something that you can commit to doing a few times per week. If exercise hasn't been a regular activity, adding five minutes of walking three days per week is a huge increase. If you have enjoyed exercise in the past, try to revisit some of the things you enjoyed doing and see if you can add them back into your routine.

Ways to get moving:

- Walking
- Stretching
- Yoga
- Biking
- Playing with children
- Hiking
- Running
- Walking the dog
- Swimming
- Tennis

- Soccer
- Skateboarding
- Surfing
- Walking to work
- Jumping rope

- Exercise video
- Dancing
- Lifting weights
- Gardening

Assert Yourself

Asserting yourself is a critical skill when you are practicing self-care. Assertiveness is a way of communicating your needs, desires, and opinions that is respectful of you and the needs and desires of others. Assertiveness distinguishes itself from aggressiveness, which only considers the needs of the aggressor, or passivity, which only considers the needs of others. When we choose to include ourselves in the things we want to prioritize in our lives, we sometimes need to say no to people who we care about or want to please. Learning how to do this will allow you to integrate and maintain your self-care practice.

Most of us are comfortable being assertive in certain contexts that don't involve people we care about or want to please. So while it is very easy to refrain from buying a car that you think is too expensive, it may be hard to tell a friend that you can't babysit her kids over the weekend. You may worry about disappointing your friend and letting her down. Those old, negative automatic thoughts and internal beliefs may surface and try to convince you that your friend won't like you anymore if you say no.

Assertive communication helps us communicate in situations like these, so we can advocate for ourselves. Rather than agreeing to do something you don't want to do and being overwhelmed and resentful, you can communicate that while you respect that she is having a hectic weekend, you are also overburdened, and it does not make sense for you to take her kids for the weekend. Assertiveness isn't a magical cure. When we assert ourselves, sometimes people may be disappointed or upset, and that's okay. In fact, if you don't experience some resistance from the other person, you probably aren't asserting yourself.

It may be helpful to consider the stressors and situations that have impacted your depression, and what might have been different if you had asserted your self-care needs. Maybe you would have turned down those extra overtime shifts at work, or not agreed to buy the expensive house your spouse really wanted that caused you a great deal of financial strain and worry. Asserting yourself in a respectful and caring way allows you to make decisions that support your health and well-being.

Eat Right

We all know that eating right impacts nearly every aspect of our physical health, but we are learning that it is also an essential component of our emotional health. A growing body of research and the evolution of a new field called "nutritional psychiatry" has found that eating a healthy diet significantly reduces our risk of becoming depressed, and can improve depression symptoms in those who are depressed. Increasing your intake of fresh fruits and vegetables, whole grains, and nuts and seeds is an important step toward feeling better. If you already eat a healthy diet, continue to do so, but if you find that you are eating a lot of sugary and fatty foods, try to add in some of these healthy foods.

When we are depressed, we sometimes crave "comfort foods" to soothe ourselves. Unfortunately, these foods often leave us feeling worse. You may find that eating a bowl of whole-grain cereal with berries may leave you feeling better than the donuts and pastries that you usually opt for. Or adding a side of veggies to your meal rather than French fries may feel like a doable substitution. Focus on adding in healthy foods rather than eliminating less-nutritious foods. Commit to eating at least five servings of fruits and vegetables every day. This simple change can have a big impact on your mental and physical health!

Nutrients that have been associated with improved depression symptoms include vitamins B_{12} and B_6, vitamin D, and omega-3 fatty acids, so try to incorporate foods high in these nutrients into your diet.

FOODS ASSOCIATED WITH DECREASED DEPRESSION	FOODS ASSOCIATED WITH INCREASED DEPRESSION
Fruits	Processed foods
Vegetables	Fried foods
Whole grains	Red and processed meats
Nuts	Refined grains (baked goods, white bread, and so on)
Seeds	
Low-fat dairy	High-fat foods
Lean meats	Refined sugar

Enjoy the Outdoors

Another simple way to improve your mood and reduce stress is spend-ing time outside in nature. Several recent studies have shown that even just a short walk in nature reduces depression and anxiety. It is unclear why being in nature has such a powerful effect on our moods, but researchers believe that the beauty, sunlight, and sounds found in nat-ural settings draw our attention outward and generate feelings of calm, well-being, and connection.

This doesn't mean you have to plan a multiday backpacking trip in the wilderness. Even just listening to nature sounds or looking at pictures of natural settings calms the fight-or-flight system. Making time to be in nature is a great way to take care of yourself. Taking a walk in a park or in your neighborhood, going to the beach, or just spending time in your garden can have real benefits. Other ideas include meeting friends for a picnic in the park, visiting local botanical gardens, reading on a park bench, or taking time in the morning to drink your coffee outside while listening to the birds.

Give Yourself Some Love

Self-compassion may be the most important skill that you cultivate in your life. Human beings are born quite vulnerable and helpless, and we rely on the care of others to grow into self-sufficient adults. We are hardwired to care for others—our offspring, family members, and community—yet the idea of caring for ourselves seems selfish and self-indulgent. This response to self-compassion reveals a bias we have against ourselves. Somehow we think we are less worthy of the compassion and care we so readily give to others. This seems very unfair and inefficient. If we have to wait for others to care for and comfort us, we are at the whims of others to meet our most basic needs! Why would we want to deny ourselves the care we can so readily give ourselves in difficult and painful moments?

Self-care and self-compassion allow you to advocate for yourself and your needs while also caring for and respecting the needs of others. We do not need to subscribe to the outdated paradigm that there are only two options: selfish or selfless. When we are selfish, we only consider our own needs, and when we are selfless, we only consider the needs of others, but there is a healthy balance in between. When we are assertive we can consider both our own needs and the needs of others.

Try to incorporate moments of self-compassion into your everyday life. When you are feeling down or hurt, take a moment to check in with yourself and see if you need some kind words of encouragement or comfort. Self-compassion expert Kristin Neff recommends that you come up with a pet name that you use for yourself (she refers to herself as "darling") when you are practicing self-compassion, or to place your hands over your heart, or to hold your own hand. You will find things that feel comfortable for you. The simplest way to summon self-compassionate words for yourself is to consider what you might say to a friend or loved one in the same situation. Funny how easy it is for us to comfort a friend, and how unnatural it feels to use the same words for ourselves.

Establishing a simple gratitude practice is also a powerful way to care for ourselves and change our thinking. Try writing three to five things that you are grateful for in your journal every day. Doing this regularly can help you get in the habit of noticing the little things in life, bringing you more joy throughout your day.

Tips for Incorporating Self-Compassion and Gratitude into Everyday Life

- Check in with yourself throughout the day and simply ask: How are you doing? What do you need?

- Notice when you see something beautiful or pleasant, and take a moment to stop and be present.

- Start a gratitude journal and write down the things you are grateful for at end of each day.

- Listen to a guided self-compassion meditation.

- Say thank you to the people in your life when they do something kind or helpful.

- Notice when you are struggling and give yourself permission to take a break and check in with yourself.

GRETA found that when she practiced self-care and self-compassion in her daily life, she could handle the inevitable setbacks or stressors with more flexibility. When her car broke down and she had to get it towed before she got to work, she was able to use compassionate self-talk and breathing exercises to calm herself. While she waited for the towing service, she decided to use the time to do a guided meditation and call a friend she hadn't spoken to in a while.

In time and with practice, Greta got better at scheduling time for herself and the things that supported her health and well-being, like going out with friends after work and making time to exercise. Some weeks were better than others, but she could recognize when she was getting off track, and steer herself back to the tools and strategies she knew would help her keep her life and mood in balance.

Key Takeaways

- Learning to prioritize yourself is a skill that will help you maintain your gains and continue to cultivate a rich and meaningful life.

- Self-care is an essential survival skill, not an occasional indulgence.

- Sometimes self-care means doing things that are "good for us" rather than doing things that "feel good."

- Self-care can happen anywhere, especially in small, private moments.

- The acronym EASE (Exercise, Assertiveness, Self-compassion, Eating) makes it easy to remember the areas of opportunity for practicing self-care.

- Regular exercise can be as effective as antidepressant medication for treating moderate depression symptoms.

- Asserting yourself and your needs is a way to advocate for yourself when you need to prioritize your health over what others might want from you.

- Eating a healthy diet and getting out in nature are important ways to improve your mood and overall health.

- Try to incorporate moments of gratitude and self-compassion into your everyday life.

chapter 10

stay the course

We have covered a lot of ground in this book. I hope that you have a new perspective on depression and strategies for managing it. Facing this challenge and making real changes to how you relate to the thoughts, feelings, and experiences takes courage and grit. I commend you for giving yourself the gift of changing your life, for taking care of yourself and cultivating compassion for the pain that depression has caused you. Now that you have the tools you need to move forward in your life, let's spend some time thinking about strategies for maintaining your gains and planning for the future.

JUAN used this book to help him understand his depression and how he could manage his symptoms by doing the things that moved him out of the vicious cycle of depression and back into his life. He had been ashamed of his negative thoughts and moods, and blamed himself for being weak and selfish. He was surprised to learn that so many people struggle with depression. He learned that his negative thinking was a symptom of depression that distorted the way he saw himself, others, and the world. When he began to challenge his distorted thoughts and recognize that they were inaccurate, he began to consider living his life in a different way. He stopped avoiding his friends and family, and integrated meditation and self-care into his life. At first, he had a really difficult time with self-compassion, but he found that he was able to begin to try to treat himself with the same compassion with which he treated his friends and family. His life was really beginning to feel more manageable, and he felt hopeful about the future.

Moving Forward

This book has covered a lot of material that will help you manage your depression and get back on track if you have a setback. If I had to choose just a handful of things that I hope you will be able to take away from this book and bring into your daily life, they would be:

- **Forgive yourself for your depression:** Depression isn't a weakness or character flaw. It is a psychiatric disorder that nearly 10 percent of us will experience in our lifetime. You are not alone, and there are many things you can do that will allow you to move through your depression and back to the things that matter to you.

- **You are not your thoughts:** Depression is characterized by a maladaptive pattern of negative thinking about ourselves, others, and the World. When we mistake these thoughts for reality, life feels understandably bleak and hopeless. Being able to identify when we are believing these negative thoughts and choosing to unhook from or challenge them is a critical CBT skill.

- **Do the opposite of what depression tells you to do:** Depression often tells us to do the opposite of what will make us feel better, like isolating ourselves from friends and family and avoiding things that might bring meaning to our lives. We can notice when we are doing this and try the "opposite reaction" instead.

- **Befriend yourself:** Self-compassion allows you to give yourself the care you would not hesitate to give to your friends and family. Don't deny yourself the benefits of your own caring and compassion. Practice self-compassion every day until it becomes second nature.

- **Practice self-care:** Do the things that will support you in continuing to feel better and do the things that matter to you. Making time for exercise, hobbies, meditation, and fun is critical to managing your mood and feeling engaged with your life.

- **When in doubt, reach out:** Social isolation is the hallmark symptom of depression. When you notice that you are isolating yourself or avoiding social interactions, remember this simple concept: When in doubt, reach out to friends and family for support.

- **Be here now:** The mindfulness skills in this book ask you to be here now, in the present moment, without judgment. Being present in the moment keeps us from ruminating on the past or worrying about the future. Practicing mindfulness throughout your day will bring you back to what you are doing, seeing, and feeling in each moment.

- **Breathe:** The simplest way to be here now is to simply shift our awareness to our breath. It is the first step in taking the necessary pause so we can respond rather than react to our thoughts and feelings. We can do this literally at any time, in any setting. Simply stop and notice your breath going in and out. Just for a few seconds, you are in the present moment. Try to do this throughout your day and see if you notice any changes.

Keep It Going

I often use the last few sessions with my patients to compile a "Greatest Hits" list. We collaborate to come up with a list of the strategies, concepts, metaphors, and insights that were particularly helpful to them. The document can become an ongoing reminder and cheat sheet to consult when there is a new challenge or setback. Greta found the following concepts and insights most helpful to her:

Greta's Greatest Hits List

1. Don't believe everything you think.

2. Distorted thinking is the fuel that feeds the depression.

3. Notice when I am catastrophizing or my thoughts are all or nothing.

4. I really can't read other people's minds! Don't believe the stories I tell myself about what other people are thinking.

5. Notice "should" and change it to "could."

6. Journaling and writing a gratitude list at night really helps.

7. I know I am shifting into negative mode when I have the thought "I am a terrible mother."

8. Progress, not perfection.

9. Use the "Identify Your Negative Automatic Thoughts" strategy when I'm catastrophizing.

10. I don't have to get everything right all of the time to be worthy or loveable.

11. It's okay to prioritize my self-care needs: exercise, meditation, time to relax.

12. Negative emotions are difficult, but I can tolerate them.

13. There is a difference between discomfort and danger.

14. Feelings are complicated and not just good or bad.

15. The STOP technique helps when I get really upset.

16. I really can tolerate not knowing sometimes.

17. Remember to be kind to myself.

18. *Breathing* is so helpful!

19. Assertion and self-care are really important skills for me!

What would be on your greatest hits list? Look through the book and your notes and exercises, and come up with a list of the ideas, skills, strategies, and insights that you learned from the book.

Signs and Signals to Watch for

Setbacks and relapses are a normal part of this process. Life will always deliver new challenges, transitions, and stressors that may lead us to revert back to old, maladaptive coping strategies. These are opportunities to strengthen your skills and build confidence that you are able to roll with life's challenges.

This is a list of things to keep an eye out for as you begin to move forward. You may want to add a few that you anticipate as well.

☐ Increased feelings of irritability or anger

☐ Thoughts of self-harm or suicide

☐ Dwelling on your negative thoughts and feelings

☐ Isolating or withdrawing from your social world

☐ Feeling checked out or disconnected

☐ Numbing yourself with substances, food, TV, or social media

☐ Putting off self-care activities

☐ Feeling overwhelmed by new life challenges

☐ Difficulty getting out of bed on several days of the week

☐ Oversleeping or not sleeping well for several days

☐ Changes in appetite (increased or decreased)

If you notice any of these signs, make sure to check in with yourself to see what may be out of balance with your life. You may want to take the depression questionnaire in chapter 2 to monitor your symptoms for a few weeks as you begin to identify what is causing the setback. This may also be a good time to consider consulting with your doctor or a trained therapist in your area (more on this in the next section). If you are having thoughts of self-harm or suicide, be sure to contact your medical doctor, go to your nearest emergency room, or call the National Suicide Prevention Lifeline at 1 (800) 273-8255.

ANTOINE had started to feel better and regain his confidence at work after reading this book and practicing the strategies. He compiled a list of things that were particularly helpful to him and planned to check in with the list every week. Nonetheless, he still felt like he might need more support managing his depression. He checked out a few of the websites mentioned in the resources section and decided to make an appointment with a therapist who specialized in CBT to continue his work managing his depression. His therapist was pleased that he already knew about CBT, and they expanded on the work he had already done on his own. He really liked having the accountability of working with the therapist and having homework to apply the skills he was learning. Eventually he just went to see her occasionally when he needed a "refresher" or was facing a new challenge.

Where Else Can I Go for Help?

This book is one of many ways to work on managing depression, but you may benefit from utilizing additional resources such as working with a therapist, joining a support group, or continuing to read about ways to take care of yourself and manage your mood. Social isolation can maintain your depression, so seeking help and support from professionals, friends, and family is very important. Learning to manage your mood and cultivate a rich life is a lifelong pursuit. The fact that you picked up this book and made it to the final chapter is a sign that you are motivated to find the resources you need to feel better and move forward in your life.

Work with a Therapist

One option for continuing your work is to work with a therapist trained in one of the CBT modalities. I have listed several places that you can go to find therapists who have been trained in CBT and other CBT modalities like MBCT (mindfulness-based cognitive behavioral therapy) and

ACT (acceptance and commitment therapy) in the resources section. I would suggest that you talk to a few therapists before you choose one. It may also make sense to speak to your medical doctor, who may know of local CBT therapists. Taking the time to talk to a few therapists and find out about their training will ensure that you find someone trained in CBT who feels like a good fit for you.

Important questions to ask a potential therapist are:

Have you been trained in CBT for depression?

Ideally, your therapist will have training from the Association for Cognitive Therapy or the Beck Institute, and will have a degree in counseling or psychology.

What will a typical session look like?

CBT tends to be a more structured and goal-oriented therapy that will follow a treatment plan that you agree to with your therapist.

How long are the sessions and how often do we meet?

A session is generally 50 minutes, and you will likely meet with the therapist weekly.

How many sessions will a typical CBT therapy take?

CBT is not meant to be a long-term therapy. I often tell my patients that it is my goal to help them become their own therapist. A typical CBT therapy will be between 16 and 24 sessions, depending on the treatment plan. People will often come back to therapy for "maintenance" sessions or to manage new challenges.

Will I have homework or activities between sessions?

CBT nearly always involves homework and the application of concepts between sessions. The most important work actually happens outside the therapy office.

How will we know if the treatment is helping?

Most CBT practitioners will use some kind of standardized questionnaire (like the one in chapter 2) to measure your depression symptoms. This allows you to monitor symptom improvement and setbacks.

Support Groups

Another way to continue CBT treatment for depression is to find a CBT for depression support group. These groups are often a more affordable option and have the additional benefit of letting you interact with others who are also learning to manage depression. You can consult the resources at the back of the book to find support groups in your area. There are also a few online support groups referenced in the resources section if you can't find a group in your area.

Key Takeaways

- It is important to spend some time thinking about strategies for maintaining your gains and planning for the future. Compile a list of the strategies, concepts, and insights that were particularly helpful to you that you can consult when there is a new challenge or setback.

- Setbacks and relapses are a normal part of this process. Life will always deliver new challenges and transitions that may lead us to revert back to old, maladaptive coping strategies.

- If you notice any of the signs or symptoms of a depression relapse, consider what might be out of balance with your life and if you need additional support.

- Consider finding a therapist or support group to continue developing your CBT skills for managing depression.

- If you are having thoughts of self-harm or suicide, be sure to contact your medical doctor, go to your nearest emergency room, or call the National Suicide Prevention Lifeline at **1 (800) 273-8255.**

resources

FINDING A THERAPIST:

Academy of Cognitive and Behavioral Therapies
AcademyofCT.org/search/custom.asp?id=4410
A database of qualified cognitive therapists who are members of
the Academy of Cognitive Therapy.

Anxiety and Depression Association of America (ADAA)
Members.ADAA.org/page/FATMain?
This website enables you to search for therapists that specialize in
CBT by specialty, insurance accepted, and zip code.

Association for Behavioral and Cognitive Therapies
ABCTCentral.org
This website allows you to search for therapists that specialize in CBT
by specialty, insurance accepted, and zip code.

Association for Contextual Behavioral Science
ContextualScience.org/civicrm/profile?gid=17&reset=1&force=1
This website features a directory of ACBS members trained in ACT.

Psychology Today
PsychologyToday.com/us/therapists
This is a database of therapists that can be searched by specialty,
insurance accepted, and zip code.

FINDING SUPPORT GROUPS:

Anxiety and Depression Association of America (ADAA)
ADAA.org/supportgroups
This website provides information about CBT support groups
by region.

Psychology Today CBT Support Group Directory
PsychologyToday.com/us/groups/cognitive-behavioral-cbt
A searchable database of CBT support groups by zip code.

DEPRESSION:

Anxiety and Depression Association of America (ADAA)
ADAA.org
ADAA provides current news and research on anxiety and depression treatment for therapists and individuals.

Association for Behavioral and Cognitive Therapies
ABCTCentral.org
ABCT provides extensive information on current depression research and treatment. The Beck Institute https://beckinstitute.org An international CBT resource for training and therapy.

National Institute of Mental Health
NIMH.NIH.gov/health/topics/depression/index.shtml
NIMH provides education and support to individuals and family members with mental health issues.

National Suicide Prevention Hotline
1 (800) 273-TALK (8255), or
SuicidePreventionLifeline.org
National Suicide Prevention Lifeline is a network of 160 call stations across the United States that provides 24/7 crisis support for individuals in distress.

MINDFULNESS AND SELF-COMPASSION:

Mindfulness-Based Cognitive Therapy
MBCT.com
Information and resources on mindfulness-based cognitive therapy.

Self-Compassion
self-compassion.org
Dr. Kristen Neff's website has extensive information and resources on self-compassion.

GUIDED MEDITATION:

Headspace
Headspace.com
Website and free or paid app for everyday meditation and mindfulness.

Insight Timer
InsightTimer.com
Website and free app with more than 45,000 guided meditations.

appendix

Thought Record

SITUATION	*Describe what was happening—who was there, what were you doing, where, when, and why?*
THOUGHTS	*Describe thoughts, images, or memories that came up for you in this situation.*
FEELINGS	*What feelings came up for you? Feel free to consult the list on page 75.*
THINKING ERROR	*Are you using one of the common thinking errors from the list on page 34-35?*
ALTERNATIVE THOUGHTS	*Is there an alternative way to look at this situation?*
OUTCOME	*Does this change how you think or behave in this situation?*

references

CHAPTER 1

American Psychiatric Association. *Diagnostic and Statistical Manual of Mental Disorders.* 5th ed. Arlington, VA: American Psychiatric Association, 2013.

Beck, Aaron T. *Cognitive Therapy of Depression.* New York: Guilford Press, 1979.

Beck Institute for Cognitive Behavior Therapy. "What Is Cognitive Behavioral Therapy (CBT)?" Beck Institute. Accessed May 16, 2015. BeckInstitute.org/get -informed/what-is-cognitive-therapy.

Beck, Judith S. *Cognitive Behavior Therapy: Basics and Beyond.* 2nd ed. New York: Guilford Press, 2011.

Dobson, Keith S. "Cognitive Therapy for Depression." In *Adapting Cognitive Therapy for Depression: Managing Complexity and Comorbidity*, edited by Mark A. Whisman, 3–35. New York: Guilford Press, 2008.

Driessen, Ellen, and Steven D. Hollon. "Cognitive Behavioral Therapy for Mood Disorders: Efficacy, Moderators and Mediators." *Psychiatric Clinics of North America* 33, no. 3 (September 2010): 537–55. doi.org/10.1016/j.psc.2010.04.005.

Greenberg, Paul E., Andree-Anne Fournier, Tammy Sisitsky, Crystal T. Pike, and Ronald C. Kessler. "The Economic Burden of Adults with Major Depressive Disorder in the United States (2005 and 2010)." *Journal of Clinical Psychiatry* 76, no. 2 (February 2015): 155–62. doi.org/10.4088/JCP.14m09298.

Hayes, Steven C., Michael E. Levin, Jennifer Plumb-Vilardaga, Jennifer L. Villatte, and Jacqueline Pistorello. "Acceptance and Commitment Therapy and Contextual Behavioral Science: Examining the Progress of a Distinctive Model of Behavioral and Cognitive Therapy."

Behavior Therapy 44, no. 2 (June 2013): 180–98. doi.org/10.1016/j
.beth.2009.08.002.

Hofmann, Steven. G., Any Asnaani, Imke J. J. Vonk, Alice T. Sawyer, and
Angela Fang. "The Efficacy of Cognitive Behavioral Therapy: A Review
of Meta-analyses." *Cognitive Therapy and Research* 36, no. 5
(October 2012): 427–40. doi.org/10.1007/s10608-012-9476-1.

Hollon, Steven D., Robert J. Derubeis, Jan Fawcett, Jay D. Amsterdam,
Richard C. Shelton, John Zajecka, Paula R. Young, and Robert Gallop.
"Effect of Cognitive Therapy with Antidepressant Medications vs
Antidepressants Alone on the Rate of Recovery in Major Depressive
Disorder." *JAMA Psychiatry* 71, no. 10 (October 2014): 1157–64.
doi.org/10.1001/jamapsychiatry.2014.1054.

Kessler, Ronald C., Wai Tat Chiu, Olga Demler, and Ellen E. Walters. "Prevalence, Severity, and Comorbidity of Twelve-Month DSM-IV Disorders
in the National Comorbidity Survey Replication (NCS-R)." *Archives of
General Psychiatry* 62, no. 6 (June 2005): 617–27. doi.org/10.1001
/archpsyc.62.6.617.

Mennin, Douglas S., Kristen K. Ellard, David M. Fresco, and James J.
Gross. "United We Stand: Emphasizing Commonalities Across
Cognitive-Behavioral Therapies." *Behavior Therapy* 44, no. 2
(March 2013): 234–48. doi.org/10.1016/j.beth.2013.02.004.

National Center for PTSD. "PTSD Basics." U.S. Department of Veterans
Affairs. Updated June 8, 2020. www.PTSD.va.gov/understand/what
/ptsd_basics.asp.

National Institute of Mental Health. "Bipolar Disorder." National Institutes
of Health. Last modified November 2017. NIMH.NIH.gov/health
/statistics/prevalence/bipolar-disorder-among-adults.shtml.

National Institute of Mental Health. "Major Depression." National
Institutes of Health. Last modified February 2019. NIMH.NIH.gov
/health/statistics/prevalence/major-depression-among-adults.shtml.

WISQARS™—Web-based Injury Statistics Query and Reporting System
(data years 2011, 2013). Centers for Disease Control and Prevention.
CDC.gov/injury/wisqars/index.html.

World Health Organization. "Depression." Last modified February 2017. WHO.int/news-room/fact-sheets/detail/depression.

World Health Organization. *The Global Burden of Disease: 2004 Update.* Geneva, Switzerland: WHO Press, 2008. WHO.int/healthinfo/global _burden_disease/2004_report_update/en.

CHAPTER 3

Beck, Aaron T. *Cognitive Therapy and the Emotional Disorders.* New York: International Universities Press, 1976.

Beck, Aaron T. *Depression: Clinical, Experimental, and Theoretical Aspects.* New York: Harper & Row, 1967.

Beck, Aaron T. "The Current State of Cognitive Therapy: A 40-Year Retrospective." *Archives of General Psychiatry* 62 (2005): 953–9.

Beck, Judith S. *Cognitive Behavior Therapy: Basics and Beyond.* 2nd ed. New York: Guilford Press, 2011.

Blackledge, John T. *Cognitive Defusion in Practice: A Clinician's Guide to Assessing, Observing, and Supporting Change in Your Client.* Oakland, CA: Context Press, 2015.

Burns, David D. *Feeling Good: The New Mood Therapy.* New York: Penguin Books, 1981.

David, Daniel, Ioana Cristea, and Stefan G. Hofmann. "Why Cognitive Behavioral Therapy Is the Current Gold Standard of Psychotherapy." *Frontiers in Psychiatry* 9, no. 4 (January 2018). doi.org/10.3389 /fpsyt.2018.00004.

Dobson, Keith S. "Cognitive Therapy for Depression." In *Adapting Cognitive Therapy for Depression: Managing Complexity and Comorbidity*, edited by Mark A. Whisman, 3–35. New York: Guilford Press, 2008.

Linehan, Marsha M. *DBT Skills Training Manual.* 2nd ed. New York: Guilford Press, 2014.

Oswald, Margit E. and Stefan Grosjean. "Confirmation Bias." In *Cognitive Illusions: A Handbook on Fallacies and Biases in Thinking,*

Judgement and Memory, edited by Rüdiger F. Polh, 79–96. Hove, UK: Psychology Press, 2004.

Somov, Pavel G. *Present Perfect: A Mindfulness Approach to Letting Go of Perfectionism and the Need for Control.* Oakland, CA: New Harbinger Publications, 2010.

CHAPTER 4

Greenberger, Dennis, and Christine A. Padesky. *Mind Over Mood: A Cognitive Therapy Treatment Manual for Clients.* New York: Guilford Press, 1995.

CHAPTER 5

Drucker, Peter F. *The Practice of Management.* New York: Harper & Row, 1954.

Drummond, Tom. *Vocabulary of Emotions/Feelings.* Handout, n.d. TomDrummond.com/leading-and-caring-for-children/emotion-vocabulary.

Prinz, Jesse. "Which Emotions Are Basic?" In *Emotion, Evolution, and Rationality*, edited by Dylan Evans and Pierre Cruse, 69–88. Oxford: Oxford University Press, 2004.

Storm, Christine, and Tom Storm. "A Taxonomic Study of the Vocabulary of Emotions." *Journal of Personality and Social Psychology* 53, no. 4 (October 1987): 805–16. doi.org/10.1037/0022-3514.53.4.805.

CHAPTER 6

Hayes, Steven C., Kirk D. Strosahl, and Kelly G. Wilson. *Acceptance and Commitment Therapy: An Experiential Approach to Behavior Change.* New York: Guilford Press, 1999.

John, Oliver P. and James J. Gross. "Healthy and Unhealthy Emotion Regulation: Personality Processes, Individual Differences, and Life Span Development." *Journal of Personality* 72: 1301-1334 (December 2004). doi.org/10.1111/j.1467-6494.2004.00298.x.

Kuyken, Willem, Ed Watkins, Emily Holden, Kat White, Rod S. Taylor, Sarah Byford, Alison Evans, Sholto Radford, John D. Teasdale, and Tim Dalgleish. "How Does Mindfulness-Based Cognitive Therapy Work?" *Behaviour Research and Therapy* 48, no. 11 (November 2010): 1105–12. doi.org/10.1016/j.brat.2010.08.003.

Remen, Rachel Naomi. *My Grandfather's Blessings: Stories of Strength, Refuge, and Belonging.* New York: Riverhead Books, 2001.

Weil, Andrew. *Health and Healing.* New York: Houghton Mifflin Harcourt, 1995.

CHAPTER 7

Hayes, Steven C., Jason B. Luoma, Frank W. Bond, Akihiko Masuda, and Jason Lillis. "Acceptance and Commitment Therapy: Model, Processes and Outcomes." *Behaviour Research and Therapy* 44: 1–25 (January 2006). doi.org/10.1016/j.brat.2005.06.006.

Plumb, Jennifer C., Ian Stewart, Joanne Dahl, and Tobias Lundgren. "In Search of Meaning: Values in Modern Clinical Behavior Analysis." *The Behavior Analyst* 32, no. 1 (March 2009): 85–103. doi.org/10.1007/bf03392177.

CHAPTER 8

Kuyken, Willem, Ed Watkins, Emily Holden, Kat White, Rod S. Taylor, Sarah Byford, Alison Evans, Sholto Radford, John D. Teasdale, and Tim Dalgleish. "How Does Mindfulness-Based Cognitive Therapy Work?" *Behaviour Research and Therapy* 48, no. 11 (November 2010): 1105–12. doi.org/10.1016/j.brat.2010.08.003.

Linehan, Marsha M. *Cognitive-Behavioral Therapy of Borderline Personality Disorder.* New York: Guilford Press, 1993.

Wohl, Michael J. A., Timothy A. Pychyl, and Shannon H. Bennett. "I Forgive Myself, Now I Can Study: How Self-Forgiveness for Procrastinating Can Reduce Future Procrastination." *Personality and Individual Differences* 48, no. 7 (May 2010): 803–8. doi.org/10.1016/j.paid.2010.01.029.

CHAPTER 9

Miller, Michael Craig. "Is Exercise a Good Treatment for Depression?" *Harvard Mental Health Letter*, June 2003.

Murri, Martino Belvederi, Panteleimon Ekkekakis, Marco Magagnoli, Domenico Zampogna, Simone Cattedra, Laura Capobianco, Gianluca Serafini, Pietro Calcagno, Stamatula Zanetidou, and Mario Amore. "Physical Exercise in Major Depression: Reducing the Mortality Gap While Improving Clinical Outcomes." *Frontiers in Psychiatry* 9 (January 2019). doi.org/10.3389/fpsyt.2018.00762.

index

A

Acceptance, 77, 123–124, 126
Antidepressants, 15–16
Assertiveness, 138–139, 143
Atypical depression, 9
Awareness, 92. *See also* Mindfulness

B

Beck, Aaron, 10, 33
Behavioral activation
  about, 113–117, 128
  eliminating activities that make you
    feel worse, 119–121
  productivity, 126–127
  scheduling pleasurable activities,
    117–119, 128
  task lists, 121–122, 128
Behavioral experiments, 60–61
Behaviors. *See also* Behavioral
  activation; Goals
  in the CBT model, 10–14
  procrastination, 122–127, 128
  STOP technique, 80–81
Beliefs
  challenging with evidence, 58–60
  challenging with experiments,
    60–61
  changing, 56–58
  identifying, 51–55, 62
  if/then traps, 55–56
  internal, 47–51, 62

Body scan, 94–95
Breathing
  4-7-8 technique, 93–94
  meditation, 88–89

C

Carnegie, Dale, 120
Cognitive behavioral therapy (CBT),
  9–14, 18, 86–87, 150–152

D

Depression
  about, 7–8
  dealing with relapses, 149–150, 153
  factors contributing to, 6–7
  management strategies,
    146–149, 153
  medications for, 15–16
  prevalence of, 4, 18
  self-assessment, 21–24
  symptoms of, 5–6
  types of, 8–9
Diet and nutrition, 139–140, 143
Distorted thinking, 8, 33–35, 40–41, 45.
  See also Beliefs
Doran, George T., 107
Downward arrow technique,
  51–55, 62

E

EASE acronym, 135, 143

Ellis, Albert, 10

Emotions. *See* Feelings and emotions

Exercise, 137–138, 143

Experiential avoidance, 13, 18

F

Fears, 43–44

Feelings and emotions

    avoidance of, 68–70, 73–74, 82

    in the CBT model, 10–14

    emotional regulation, 76–79, 82

    identifying, 70–72

    labeling, 74–76

    mindfulness and, 92–93, 96

    negative, 67–68, 82

    STOP technique, 80–81

    thoughts and, 29–33, 38, 44–45

Fight, flight, or freeze response, 68–70

G

Goals

    overcoming obstacles to, 108–111

    setting, 102–104, 111

    SMART, 106–108

    SMART goals, 111

    and values, 104–106

Gratitude, 141–142

Grief, 7

Grounding, 90

H

How to Make Friends and Influence
    People (Carnegie), 120

I

If/then traps, 55–56

L

Life domains, 104–106

M

Major depressive disorder (MDD), 8

Medications, 15–16

Meditation

    body scan, 94–95

    breathing, 88–89

    mountain, 93

Mindfulness, 17

    about, 85–88, 96

    body scan, 94–95

    breathing meditation, 88–89

    and emotional experiences, 92–93, 96

    exercises, 90–92

    4-7-8 breathing technique, 93–94

Mindfulness-based cognitive therapy
    (MBCT), 86–87

Monoamine oxidase inhibitors
    (MAOIs), 16

My Grandfather's Blessings
    (Remen), 92

N

National Suicide Prevention Lifeline, 6,
    150, 153

Nature, 140

Neff, Kristin, 141

Negative confirmation bias, 39–40

Normalizing, 77, 124, 126

Nutritional psychiatry, 139

O

Opposite action, 113, 115

P

Pain, 87
Persistent depressive disorder (PDD), 8
Postpartum depression (PPD), 9
Predictions, 43–44, 60–61
Premenstrual dysphoric disorder
    (PMDD), 9
Present, being, 86–88
Procrastination, 122–127, 128

R

Remen, Rachel Naomi, 92
Rules, 60–61

S

Sadness, 7
Seasonal affective disorder (SAD), 9
Selective serotonin reuptake
    inhibitors (SSRIs), 15
Self-assessment, 21–24
Self-care. See also Self-compassion
    assertiveness, 138–139, 143
    defined, 133, 143
    eating right, 139–140, 143
    exercise, 137–138, 143
    nature, 140
    practicing, 134–136
    sleep, 135–136
Self-compassion, 78, 124, 126,
    140–142
Serotonin and norepinephrine
    reuptake inhibitors (SNRIs), 15
Setbacks, 149–150, 153
Situational depression, 8
Sleep, 135–136
SMART goals, 106–108, 111
STOP technique, 80–81

Suffering, 87
Suicidal thoughts, 5–6, 150, 153
Support groups, 152
Symptoms, of depression, 5–6.
    See also Self-assessment

T

TANS acronym, 76–79, 123–126, 128
Teasdale, J., 86
Therapists, 150–152
Thinking errors, 8, 34–35, 40–41, 45.
    See also Beliefs
Thoughts. See also Beliefs
    in the CBT model, 10–14, 31
    charged, 40
    fears, 43–44
    and Feelings and emotions, 29–33,
        38, 44–45
    negative, 36–40, 42–43
    predictions, 43–44
    records, 37–38
    restructuring, 77, 123, 125–126
    thinking errors, 8, 34–35, 40–41, 45
Tricyclic antidepressants, 16

V

Values, 104–106

W

Walking, mindful, 91
Weil, Andrew, 93

acknowledgments

I would like to thank the many people who have contributed to the completion of this book. To my extraordinarily loving and patient husband, Oliver, for supporting me while I finished this book during the COVID-19 sheltering-in period. I would also like to thank my two wonderful daughters, Simone and Katya, who inspire me every day.

I cannot overemphasize the importance of the professional and clinical support I receive from my partners at the San Francisco Bay Area Center for Cognitive Therapy. I am so grateful to benefit from the legacy of the oldest center for cognitive therapy in the Bay Area, which just celebrated its 25th anniversary. Special thanks to Michael Tompkins, who has provided so much encouragement and support to me. I would also like to thank my partners at the Center: Joan Davidson, Daniela Owen, Jonathan Barkin, and Emily Berner.

I am very grateful to Dr. Allison Harvey and the staff at Golden Bear Mood and Research Clinic, where I received extraordinary training and supervision in CBT for depression and insomnia. Special thanks to the excellent supervision and support from Dr. Steven Hollon.

Lastly, I want to thank the many individuals I have treated in my practice over the years. I treasure the knowledge and inspiration I have gained from the people who have been willing to work with me to improve their lives in profound ways. You are why I love my work and wanted to write this book. Thank you.

about the author

Monique Thompson, PsyD, (PSY 25685) is a licensed clinical psychologist. Dr. Thompson received a master's degree from the University of Pennsylvania and a doctoral degree in clinical psychology from the California School of Professional Psychology. She is a certified cognitive therapist and Diplomate of the Academy of Cognitive and Behavioral Therapies.

Dr. Thompson has extensive experience providing individualized cognitive therapy to adults and teens with depression, anxiety, and insomnia. Dr. Thompson has practiced in a variety of settings, including Kaiser Permanente, UC Berkeley, and private practice. She spent several years at the Golden Bear Mood and Sleep Research Center at UC Berkeley as a member of a treatment development team that seeks to explore and enhance cognitive therapies for depression. She has published research on memory mechanisms and interventions to improve individual therapy outcomes. She is a partner at the San Francisco Bay Area Center for Cognitive Therapy and adjunct faculty at the UC Berkeley Extension. She coauthored a book on teen insomnia with Dr. Michael Tompkins, *The Insomnia Workbook for Teens* (New Harbinger, 2019).

CPSIA information can be obtained
at www.ICGtesting.com
Printed in the USA
BVHW091010301020
592126BV00005B/5

9 781647 391003